THE SLENDER REED

THE SAGA OF GREED AND VENGEANCE
THAT THE PEOPLE ARE TOLD IS JUSTICE

JOHN W. CASSELL

INKWATER
PRESS

Publisher: Inkwater Press | www.inkwaterpress.com

Paperback
ISBN-13 978-1-59299-739-8 | ISBN-10 1-59299-739-2

Printed in the U.S.A.
All paper is acid free and meets all ANSI standards for archival quality paper.

1 3 5 7 9 10 8 6 4 2

To my new friends in Wales: Lee, Becky and Lucy.... And to all others concerned or just curious about systems of justice and their operation....as well as to all those who worked with me in my over a quarter century in law enforcement this book is humbly dedicated

TO THE BROTHERS I'VE BURIED...
MAY GOD GRANT THEM PEACE

Sherman Toler .... NMSP [shot to death in traffic stop]

Manuel Olivas .... NMSP [killed by drunk driver]

Glen Huber.. NMSP [shot to death at domestic disturbance]

Lowell Howard ....NMSP [killed in plane crash]

David Smith ....NMSP [killed in plane crash]

Pete Ross........ NMSP [died from injuries caused by crash of federal helicopter in drug raid]

Sa Fuimaono .... ASDPS [drowned searching for murder victim]

Liusila Brown ....ASDPS [shot to death unarmed outside courthouse]

Table of Contents

Characters

Herb ....Herb's Guns & Ammo
Linda Sue Kristley.. Linda Sue's Café
Dr. Stanley Broward .... Clinical psychologist
Lisa Rockwell.. Defense Attorney
Allie Cairns .... Restaurant Owner
Bud Weston.. Weston's Food and Dairy
Gwenn Cranford..Ed's wife
Chris Cranford.. Ed's son
Lupe Cranford ....Ed's daughter
Stacy Cranford ....Ed's newborn daughter

STATE'S ATTORNEY'S OFFICE

EDWARD ANTONY CRANFORD........... State's Attorney

Barry Silverman...................................... Deputy State's Attorney
Paul Evans Feingold ....Assistant State's Attorney
Susan Toulouse.....................................Assistant State's Attorney
Karen Dillard .... Head Secretary
Marian Whiting... Budget, Reception
Barbara Keating............................Victim Witness Coordinator
Marty Droud..Diversion counselor
Vickie Morris ....Secretary
Harry Kinney .... investigator
Louie Gabaldón .... investigator

JUDICIARY

Barbara Peterson Graves..**Clerk of the Superior Court**

Millie Freeman .... Doris Sanchez
Filomena Urioste

The Hon. Anastasio Miguel Santestevan .... Division I Superior Court
Estrellita Gonzales .... division secretary
Gregorio 'Honcho' Lerida .... bailiff
Lori Michaels .... courtroom deputy

The Hon. Eric Geoffrey Cronin .... Division II Superior Court
Celestine Ramirez .... division secretary
Tim Slidell .... bailiff
Allyson Koury .... courtroom deputy

The Hon. Gilbert Maynard Beecham .... Division III Superior Court
Ashley Cresswell Urioste .... division secretary
Richard Dickens .... bailiff
Sylvia Strachmann .... courtroom deputy

GARFIELD COUNTY SHERIFF'S OFFICE

Mike Townsend   Sheriff
Dave Moss   Herb Marshall
Sgt. Hugh Jasper   Alex Jaramillo

STATE HIGHWAY PATROL

Captain Harold Renfro   Ptl Jack Lawson
Lt. Wesley Brown   Ptl Marv Hanlon
Ptl Steve Grimes
Det. Jeremy Dickson

URIOSTE SPRINGS POLICE

Enrique Guadalupe   **Marcelino Urioste Seguín**
D/C Hansdieter 'Fritz' Strachmann   Ronni Bliss-secretary
Ptl Danny Steele   Ptl. Tim Blackwell
Lt. Roger Burke   Ptl. Carlos Segura
Sgt. Tyrone Washington
Ptl. Leroy White
Capt. Dave Haller

GARFIELD COUNTY SOCIAL SERVICES

Mindy 'Mad Dog' Schellenberger-director

Seferino Lopez   Geraldine Capehart

Johnny Washington   Filomena Garcia

GARFIELD COUNTY PROBATION SERVICES

Howard Martin Creeley-director

Lillian Greene   Martín Urioste

Kyle Kerbow   Arturo Martinez

FEDERAL HEAT

Paula Winters.......................... Assistant United States Attorney

S/A Carl Smallwood .... FBI

S/A Julian DeWitt .... FBI

Foreword

It would be hard to devote the best working years of one's life, not to mention the marriage and stomach lining that paid the price, to a system or process without coming away with some very strong feelings about it and its participants.

In this regard I am no different than anyone else, though I am happy to say that the recording of such an outlook as well as a marshaling of the pertinent facts supporting it is much too large a task to even begin in a volume of this size.

Instead, I think of this volume as I do all my other works, as an attempt at story telling calculated by its authenticity to provide meaningful entertainment for the reader, rather than carry a cross or try everyone's patience with an agenda or point of view.

In fact, I can say at the outset of this project that I knew and associated with good cops and bad cops, good lawyers and bad lawyers, and indeed a system that worked as it should as well as one that did not.

What I hope the reader finds within these pages are some realistic travails…and blessings… that one in the position of the characters could expect to find working in the American system of justice in 1981 [a year I picked at random in lieu of any one of the twenty-five that saw me working as a trial prosecutor].

My feelings on the process itself are reserved for other venues, though as anyone knows, things are changing so fast in practically every walk of life nowadays that the well developed, tested by bitter and happy experience opinions and outlooks that I carried away from my career were likely out of date and irrelevant years before I put pen to paper and created **The Slender Reed**.

So with this in mind I hope that what will emerge for the reader is a look at some aspects of the system not necessarily encountered in intellectual discussions. Aspects which while they might to some degree be food for thought will mainly provide a journey of enjoyment.

Chapter One

Just Another Lamb To The Slaughter

Saturday February 26, 1981: 4th and Alamo Streets, Urioste Springs

A carnival atmosphere prevailed on all sides of the Urioste Springs Police Station. The cable news station was there, attracting half the town to shout and wave at the cameras. City police sentinels holding shotguns were posted at the door. The Highway Patrol's Tactical Response Team was there, dressed in black combat gear and body armor, wearing black helmets with visors and carrying assault rifles. Their special weapons support was there as well. Behind the barricade of cars on the west side of the station one could see a battering ram, several grenade launchers with the telltale blue canisters already loaded and a flamethrower in the final moments of assembly by an officer wearing a space suit…the suit that enabled a man to walk through fire.

At the far end of the north side parking lot were the VIP observers. Captain Harold Renfro of the Highway Patrol was watching while he talked into the police radio in his car. He had briefed the TRT earlier, then come on scene to pull out his men who had conducted a loose quarantine of the area for the past three days.

Also present and standing next to the Captain, his eyes riveted on the deadly force that had been mustered by the State Highway Patrol in response to his summons, was Garfield County's chief law enforcement officer, State's Attorney Edward A. Cranford. His shoulders were stooped from exhaustion, but his face was alive, practically burning with a new found self-esteem, something tragically missing from the experienced prosecutor for nearly the last two months.

But it was back now, the State's Attorney riding the crest of exhilaration generated by a noble, courageous assault on the powerbrokers of corruption, cruelty and decay. Every lawman has a limit of the despair he can take before he must swallow his gun or start fighting back. For the past three days Cranford was energized with that righteous anger that only someone watching his life's work being flushed down the toilet can know.

It hadn't been easy… Lord knows it hadn't been easy. There was a long lonesome valley he had to walk first… a passage darkened by fear and depression… by self-doubt so formidable he often felt that death was his only way out.

No… it hadn't been easy… not at all…

The opening minutes of 1981

Probably the biggest advantage a State's Attorney had over a moderately successful private attorney was a radio car. Cranford was certain of it. Nothing exorbitant, mind you. Just your basic black Ford sedan. Certainly not a Cadillac like the Governor or Lieutenant Governor. This was as it should be. After all, there was a state's attorney for each county. It wasn't like there was only one or even five in the whole state.

Not even white wall tires graced this vehicle with the official plates showing front and rear as it slowly poked its way along snow-packed All Wars Memorial Boulevard in the heart of Urioste Springs. Not that Urioste Springs *had* a heart. The sole occupant of the black, law enforcement radio equipped Ford, Edward Antony Cranford, had thus far been unable to find one. But then who, where or what did?

The snow had begun eight hours ago. Delivered c.o.d. to Urioste Springs in one of those gale-force storms that would roll off the prairie and dump on the first settlement that got in its way. The storm had since gone about its business, out of respect for all the drunks that planned to turn the area streets and highways into first class carnage this holiday night. Now the snow was falling gently, peacefully, covering this monument to the wrecked dreams of three groups of people with the same white blanket that worked so well in Cranford's Philadelphia youth.

The Ford reached the end of the Boulevard…. the dead end into Topeka Way. Named for the railroad it once shadowed, this potholed pathway ran west to Main Street with its courthouse and a few businesses that stubbornly hung on to the once proud downtown location, Alamo Street with the city police station, then on past the sprawling Cesar Chavez housing project, further past a trailer park here and there and the district office of the State Highway Patrol, past the brooding black void that once was home to [maybe a division or so of] the Army, then finally to the highway.

The courthouse, still festooned with Christmas lights, was home to Cranford and his staff, the judiciary, county prisoners [at the very top] and the Garfield County Sheriff's Office.

Cranford avoided the tug on his perforated ulcer the courthouse had strangely been delivering for the past six hours or so by turning the Ford left…eastward…onto the potholed pathway that ran past the small but proud single unit dwellings built by the railroad laborers, past the black void that once was the railroad yard, then on out the highway to the Atlantic-Richfield truck stop, then onward past irrigated farmlands to the east and ranch and range country to the south.

The radio was cranking up. Two city units were already out with two separate suspected drunk drivers on the north end of town. A sheriff's vehicle had one stop going to the west. A violent domestic had the rest of the city units at what the cops called "Cesar's Palace".

To the east the Highway Patrol was running a major sobriety roadblock. Cranford had promised Lieutenant Wesley Brown he'd swing by there later. Brown was one of his favorites. A fourteen year veteran of police work, he miraculously managed to be habitually cheerful in outlook and happily married besides. When the "Roots" craze hit he applied his investigative skills to his origins and found to his immense pride he was of Bantu chiefly stock. He had cut his teeth in the state's central urban sprawl, a beat demanding sharpened street cop instincts. Challenging as it was, Brown had a leg up in that he grew up on some of its meaner streets. The man was clearly a comer, and in every respect a positive counterweight to the city's legendary 'Black Mariah,' Deputy Chief Hansdieter "Fritz" Strachmann.

Cranford wasn't ready for the roadblock yet, in fact he wasn't ready for much of anything except maybe some biscuits and gravy at Linda Sue's Café, a greasy spoon in the 300 block of East Topeka Way. His ulcer was starting to act up as he became increasingly aware of the nasty curve a cruel fate had tossed him.

When he took himself to law school on his GI Bill, he felt things couldn't be turning out better, particularly since midway through its course of study he had finally persuaded the darkly beautiful love of his life, Gwenn Gutierrez, to marry him. The wedding ended an almost decade-long pursuit, a pursuit paused only briefly by a disastrous marriage resulting in a vicious divorce and aftermath.

Gwenn had lost her first husband to the Vietnam War. Despite the almost impossible job-to Cranford anyway- of raising on her own the little boy and girl born of the marriage, Gwenn had gotten herself through college and was holding down a responsible job in an anti-poverty program in the state capital. Gwenn was born and raised there at a time the town was little more than thirty thousand people and as many tumbleweeds. In one of those storybook twists of fate, Cranford had been invited to the home of his best friend at the state university, Roberto Gutierrez, for Thanksgiving dinner. Gwenn was his kid sister and a junior in high school at the time.

With Gwenn at his side, Cranford graduated law school with honors, passed the bar exam, and began his career with the State Criminal Investigations Bureau in Gwenn's home town, the capital. As the first three years of their marriage passed, however, cultural differences began to result in friction between the couple. Gwenn was part of a large, close-knit family. Her children, who Cranford loved and raised as his own, were very close to their grandmother, while Gwenn also enjoyed spending time at her family home.

Ed Cranford, on the other hand, came from a broken home and small family. At age 17 he left home to go west to college. While maintaining a love for his family, it was observed more often at a distance than close up. He believed that a marriage should create a new familial focus for its members. By 1977 the impasse had become acute. Cranford decided some space was needed between his house-hold and Gwenn's parental home.

He had investigated several cases with the help of Lieutenant Brown, and it was through Brown he became acquainted with the man considered by many to be the most respected state's attorney of them all, Gilbert Maynard Beecham of Urioste Springs. The two men hit it off from the beginning, so it wasn't long before the Cranfords moved there with Edward trading his CIB badge for that of an assistant state's attorney.

With Beecham as a mentor, Cranford's own trial reputation took root and grew. As the Highway Patrol began making some spectacular seizures of Columbian cocaine, he began tangling on search and seizure cases with lawyers listing offices in both Miami and Bogotá. Gwenn meanwhile became pregnant and it began to appear the family was taking root in their new community. When veteran Deputy State's Attorney Arthur Leslie retired, Cranford was appointed by Beecham to take his place.

In actuality the marriage was imperiled. Gwenn missed her family, a condition only exacerbated by Ed's twelve hour work days followed by a return home exhausted and uncommunicative, then his handling emergency calls often all through the night. The couple's third child, and first of their marriage, was born while Ed was in court.

For his part, Cranford often felt deserted by Gwenn. His job required him to keep many state secrets, and the problems posed by his heavy caseload made him even more uncommunicative as he pondered them through his evenings and weekends at home. He was paged out of his adoptive daughter's First Communion Mass to handle a high profile murder. Always careful to keep his family from being visually identified with him, except to go to church and breakfasts on Sunday mornings, he nonetheless found himself confronted by the hysterical and angry mother of someone he had sent to prison while out with his small adoptive son Chris one weekday morning.

Cranford's refuge increasingly became his job, and yet as Deputy State's Attorney, the number two man in the office, he increasingly found himself at odds with Urioste Springs' most powerful and distinguished citizen, Chief of Police Enrique Guadalupe Marcelino Urioste Seguín.

Born to wealth and social position, a direct descendant of the city's founding clan, suave and urbane to the core, Chief Urioste nonetheless was tough as nails. He enlisted in the Marine Corps and saw action in the Korean War. After completing his hitch, he went to the state university, ultimately graduating from its law school. He was a patrolman with the Dallas Police Department, later returning to Urioste Springs to succeed his father as chief of its police department. The combination of old money, new grit and keen intelligence made him a fearsome lobbyist for the interests of Garfield County. His friends could count on some impressive rewards, and indeed his all out lobbying efforts got State's Attorney Beecham the gift he wanted most, a Superior Court judgeship.

His enemies often wound up in prison, or otherwise were condemned to lives of disgrace. The cases that seemed to materialize out of thin air against these poor souls, who included such a diverse lot as a popular high school athletics director, a CIO union organizer, even a former sheriff of Garfield County were nonetheless facially strong. How he did it was a mystery to Cranford, though he refused a couple of cases on general ethical grounds, convinced something was wrong somewhere. With Beecham as State's Attorney there was no problem. It was, after all, his district and his call.

Yet now Cranford's boss and mentor had resigned his office to take up the judgeship created just for him through Chief Urioste's singular lobbying efforts. While it was an open secret that Urioste had tried to convince Leslie to come out of retirement and take the job, a result that would have pleased Cranford no end, Leslie had refused. Neither of the two Assistant State's Attorney's even had the minimum five years of legal practice necessary to take the top job, and Cranford had no alternative prospects lined up and with a growing family needed the paycheck more than ever.

Yes, a nasty curve had been thrown by fate at someone who had actually looked forward to going to work much of the time.

"But no longer, apparently," Cranford mumbled to himself, even as he cut the wheel to the left, taking the Ford across the two westbound lanes and coming to rest in about eight inches of snow in front of Linda Sue's virtually empty establishment.

"Howdy, Trouble ," the flirtatious cowgirl turned businesswoman drawled from behind the counter as she grabbed a menu and prepared to escort her VIP customer to his special spot out of sight of people on the street. A downtown businessman talking in hushed tones with a Garfield County deputy sheriff were the only two customers in the place in the early hours of the New Year.

Cranford waited until Sue got just past the curtain separating the table from a view of the other patrons. He pressed her tightly against the wall, holding her wrists behind her with one hand, the other forcing her face upward by the hair. His mouth closed around hers and the probing began…deep and delicious…about as heavenly as things were capable of getting for him.

Sue put up her usual vicious but quiet losing fight, with muffled pleading for extra delight. Truth be told, Sue loved a good losing fight. Ed adored the sense of struggle Sue brought to their make-outs. He could only guess how delightful the Great Motel Rendezvous would be. They bantered back and forth about it, but Sue hated the more effective forms of birth control, preferring the petite figure Ed lusted after. Ed knew that any get together within a hundred miles was a sure fire set-up for blackmail.

Stalemate.

"Money's on the table, Sue." The businessman called out.

"It better be, you ol' hoss thief!" she panted after Ed reluctantly freed her mouth.

Herb Knowles ran the downtown gun shop where Ed bought his wadcutters. Every year at Christmas Herb brought the State's Attorney a fourteen pound smoked turkey and a large tin of shelled pecans. Beecham shared the pecans with the office staff as his own perforated ulcer prevented full enjoyment. The smoked turkey he took home.

"Happy New Year, Cranford…Sue." He called just seconds before the jingling bells over the door announced his departure into the Arctic night.

Ed reached for the top button on Sue's blouse.

"Dave hasn't left," Sue whispered as she stopped him.

Deputy Sheriff Dave Moss was one of the leading marksmen in the state, hence his ongoing friendship with Herb. Trophies adorned the mantel over the fireplace in the home he shared with his wife Diane.

He was determined to add Sue to his collection of trophies. He popped through the curtain in time to watch Ed raise a coffee cup to his lips. Sue was seated at the table smoking a cigarette.

The picture of disappointment was obvious. It made Ed smile. Moss was a real bastard when it came to snooping. It was rumored he had something on at least one Garfield County Commissioner. He also suspected Cranford was a rival for Sue's affection.

"You need somethin', Moss?"

"Yeah, Counselor. I wanna do a reverse sting."

Cranford let out a pained sigh. "What's your boss gonna think?"

"Well a' course he's agin it."

Sheriff Mike Townsend was straight as an arrow. A devout Baptist and one of his church's leading laymen, he was serving his fourth term. Urioste had destroyed the previous sheriff because he made the mistake of doing an undercover drug investigation that included two buys from pushers within the city limits.

Suddenly the sheriff was bouncing checks all over Urioste Springs. He swore his bank account had been tampered with. "That's what all the deadbeats say," snarled then-Captain Strachmann, who had charge of the case, in a statement to the local paper, *The Ojo Urioste*.

The case mysteriously settled with the ex-sheriff agreeing to move away and stay gone. He had some sort of job at the state law enforcement academy, some two hundred miles distant in the state capital. It was an office rumor that Beecham still had the checks in his private safe.

Sheriff Townsend's recipe for survival was simple: he kept his enforcement efforts outside the city limits. At the courthouse he ran a quiet jail. Above all, he didn't "do dope". Chief Urioste described him as a "first rate guardian of the law".

Uh huh.

"Who's gonna be your U-C Moss?"

"That's the best part, counselor!"

Cranford shook his head, the picture of weary frustration.

The Deputy's eyes narrowed. "Wh…what's the matter?"

"Look, Dave. I'm tired…it's New Year's. Come to the office with your boss…or better yet I'll come to yours."

"When? We gotta move on this one."

"I'll bet. I've got a trial on the third that's gonna plead. Anytime this week you want."

"Deal!" The Deputy slapped Cranford on the back. "I'll be back later, Sue." He winked.

"No ya won't. I'm closin'."

"When?"

"Right now, pard."

Moss wasn't used to being turned down by women. His face was the picture of shock. "What about him ?" he indicated Cranford.

"He's givin' me some legal advice."

"You ain't supposed to do that, counselor."

Cranford buried his f ace in his hands. "And *you* ain't supposed to plan drug cases behind your boss' back. Just go, Dave. We'll talk later."

"Well I sure as shit don't get this."

"Git your behind outta my joint!" Even Moss understood when Sue really meant "no".

The frustrated Don Juan literally backed out of the café with Sue practically pushing him. Cranford heard the bells, Sue's deadbolt and finally the curtains, which blotted out a view from street and sidewalk.

Dressed only in the leopard panties Cranford got her one day when especially horny, Sue padded silently back to the VIP table and sat in Cranford's lap. She poured him the last cup in the pot, then took his face in her hands.

"Ever hear of a town called Amarillo?"

"Been there many times."

"Ever hear of an eatery there called The Big Texan?"

"Ate there every chance I got."

Sue began softly kissing his face. "They got a motel there now you big lug."

"I'm game. When's a good time for you, babe?"

Sue drew back with amazement. "Well that was sure quick!"

Cranford smirked. "I guess if you call two and a half years quick."

Sue gave that vixen-like smile of hers. "It's been that long already?"

"Every bit of it."

She gave him a kiss on the mouth. "You look so careworn, darlin'." Reaching into his shirt pocket, she got him a Chesterfield, lit it and stuck it in his mouth.

Cranford took a long drag, then exhaled into a coughing fit. "Aww fuck it."

"Huh?"

"You know you're just gonna cancel at the last minute."

Sue took the cigarette from Cranford and took a drag of her own. "Well it just so happens Amarillo is host this year to the TriState Restaurant Owners Association."

"I guess one reason to cancel is as good as the next."

"And this year they are offering several workshops on help available to rebuild decaying downtowns."

"Sounds compelling."

"I've got nights free."

"Who else from this burg is going?"

"Allie Cairns of course."

"That does it."

"Everyone else is staying downtown."

"Cairns'll be on you like flies to shit."

"He'll never find me."

Cranford had learned that this cynical pose of his eased the pain…. The pain inevitably caused by Sue's cancellation. He reached in his pocket for another cigarette.

Sue again took his face in her hands. "You're not happy, are you Eddie?"

"*Happy?*"

"I don't mean this minute. I mean overall…in your life… You're just…not happy…are you?"

Cranford shrugged. "Happy as I've got a right to be, I guess."

Sue slid off his lap and stood up. "I was going to spring my big surprise on you at the motel."

"Yeah…sure."

"But I can see you need a sneak preview. Wait here." With that she padded off to the kitchen.

Cranford stood up and walked into the main part of the café, parting the curtains for a quick peek outside.

Topeka Way was a winter wonderland. Every street light revealed heavy clouds of falling snow. Damn near a foot was on the ground.

"Get in here you big lug!"

Determined to resist Sue's unusually strong promise of the long awaited, ever-cancelled motel rendezvous, Cranford practically dragged himself back to the VIP section.

At the curtains he stopped dead. Linda Sue's petite body was wrapped in the skimpiest of skimpy black lustwear, complete with black stockings on those divine legs and black heels.

"Wowwww!"

In her hands were several lengths of silken cord and a roll of duct tape. Her vixen smile lit up the planet. "Well, you old Hoss thief…. whaddaya think of your play toy now?"

Cranford swallowed as he gaped at the much too fetching sight.

Sue burst into laughter. "I've done the impossible, yessirree! A lawyer at a loss for words!"

After a couple more minutes pregnant with gaping, Cranford walked over to Sue, clamped her wrists behind her back, then marched her through the kitchen into her living quarters, stopping at the big picture mirror in her bedroom. He turned her to it.

"I want you to take a look at yourself…a *good* look at yourself,"

"How do you think I got dressed, you brute." She was actually struggling to free herself. "Come on, damn you…let me go."

"You're gonna face up to a few things first. We both are."

"What the hell brought this on?" Sue angrily asked as she struggled even harder to free her hands.

"Tonight brought this on, Sue…"

"I guess my sneak preview was a flop. Dammit LET ME GO!"

"If you don't stop struggling I'm gonna use that duct tape you so fortuitously brought in here."

"You son of a bitch! LET ME GO!"

The more she struggled, the tighter Cranford held on. After more unsuccessful pleading she finally stopped resisting. "All right… you want me helpless… So I'm helpless…you bastard."

"We're both helpless, Sue."

"You don't look it to me."

"Give it four months….then you'll see."

"You mean Urioste, don't you, Eddie?"

"Yes."

"It can't be *that* bad. Beecham held the job for years."

"I don't seem to have his tact. And yes, Sue, it can be that bad. There's a few people in prison now because they wrote a letter to the editor….tried to run for office… all sorts of things but opposed to the Chief."

Tears suddenly appeared in Sue's eyes. "So what is the point of this conversation, Eddie… I'm starting to get a really bad feeling."

"As I looked out on Topeka Way about half an hour ago, *I* started to get a really bad feeling. Suddenly it hit me…right between the eyes."

"Well you know I'm here for you, Eddie. Do you need to spend more time with me? Are you thinking of leaving Gwenn? How can I best help you through this?"

Cranford looked down as the silence became deafening.

"Oh my God….oh no."

"Please don't make it any harder than it is, Sue."

"Any *harder*? On who?" Sue fixed a look bordering on hate on the smoldering wreck standing in front of her. "Unless I've been dreaming it seems like not forty minutes or so ago we were talking about taking *us* to new heights."

"I'm sorry, Sue… more and more things are hitting me the further into the night we go… I'm sorry."

"You sure as hell *should* be, Eddie. Playing with my feelings like this." Her tears began falling. A minute or so later, she shrugged. "I always knew you weren't going to leave Gwenn, but you seemed to need love *so desperately*….my heart just went out to you."

"You've kept me going these past two and a half years, Sue."

"Yet *this* is how you treat me? You're gonna just walk out of here?"

"I'm trying to spare you…"

"Spare me *what*, Eddie? A tearful New Year?" As her tears began falling freely, she grabbed her portable mirror and smashed it against the wall over and over, covering the floor with glass shards . "Seems like I got that already, you heartless *bastard*! You *heartless BASTARD!*"

Totally winded from her exertions, Sue dropped the broken mirror onto the floor, then slowly sank to the bed.

"Sue…I…"

"Just go, Eddie…. Please….just go."

"But Sue….I want to ex…."

"You've done quite enough for one year, Eddie. Quite enough. If you stay a minute longer I won't be responsible for my actions."

. . . .

Ed Cranford drove home through snow that lay over a foot deep on the streets and continued to fall from the skies in buckets. He was hopeful that Gwenn had finished making the black-eyed peas he had seasoned and begun cooking shortly after dinner.

Since arriving in Urioste Springs, the Cranfords had staged an open house every New Year's Day. Every cop, whether on or off duty, whether city, county or state, was invited to stop by and have a cup of Ed's by now famous black-eyed peas, a snack which supposedly gave its eater good luck throughout the year.

Depending on how Gwenn had helped he could either go straight to bed or else cook for a couple more hours. Either alternative was okay with him, though the thought of bed along about now seemed especially welcome.

As he drove up to the house, he noticed Gwenn's car missing from the driveway. Since it was a bit after three a.m., and since a major winter storm was closing roads across the state, this was not a welcome sight.

Opening the door, the smell of something burning assaulted his nostrils. Running to the kitchen, he found the black-eyed peas had been turned into a solid black gunk, while the flame still burning under the pot filled the house with a noxious smell besides.

Turning off the flame, Ed went around opening windows. While doing this he saw Gwenn's note. She had taken the kids and driven over two hundred miles of treacherous roads…roads filled this particular night with more than the usual number of drunk drivers, and this in a state whose usual number was second in the nation.

She was braving these not inconsiderable hazards to visit her mom. The note also said she would likely be staying until the roads were clear.

Ed dialed the home number for the commander of the Urioste Springs office of the Highway Patrol, Captain Harold Renfro.

"Harry... Happy New Year brother."

"Same to you, Ed. Ready for that open house tomorrow?"

"Well the door will be open, but there won't be any food."

"Don't tell me you burned it! Or was it Gwenn?"

"Yes... on her way out the door to pay her mother a visit."

"Oh man, you have black eyed peas down to a fine art if I remember right."

"No...you remember right. I'm more than a little ticked about it too."

"She picked a bad time. Want us to do a welfare check?"

"Yes, I'd feel a whole lot better knowing she at least made it."

"When's she comin' back?"

"Not until the roads are clear, she says."

"Guess you got the place to yourself until Spring!"

"Yeah, that's probably when all right."

"They still on Capitol Way?"

"Yeah, same one as last time and it's still the Delta 88."

"I'll call Captain Martinez soon as we hang up."

"That'd sure be a load off my pea brain."

"Okay, bud, Happy New Year once again."

"Same to you, Harry. Lemme know when you need to create a publicly held non-profit corporation."

"I better get movin' before Urioste gets you!"

"Oh yeah, I'll be lucky to see the light of February."

"Least you won't have no more headaches!"

"Roger that, man. Chopping block is the absolute least..."

"Bet your shoes ain't too comfy right now."

"Dicey to say the least."

"Okay....I'm on it."

"Yeah…much obliged, Harry."

Too bad the roadblock wasn't still on….mighta' taken Ed's mind off a few things, but it was scrubbed due to bad weather, leaving nothing but the smell of burnt peas to sniff.

This would have been a highly difficult year even *with* Ed's traditional cup of New Year's good luck. Unfortunately he had forfeited any good luck the peas might have held *and* got Sue and Gwenn mightily pissed off besides.

Now there would be no friendly face to run to, just a hog fight at home to follow the hog fight at work until the Big Boss man pulled the plug.

This year was gonna be *loads* of fun.

Chapter Two

When the Feds Come Calling

Monday January 3, 1981: State's Attorney's Office; Garfield County Courthouse

"Everybody's ready for the staff meeting, Ed."

"Okay, Barb, thanks."

"You know Marty's a spy, don't you?"

"Yes. I wonder why Gil put spies on the payroll."

"Simple…he wanted the Boss Man to know everything was kosher."

Ed cracked a smile. Gil Beecham's deviousness never ceased to impress him.

"Oh….and the Sheriff is waiting to see you. Says it's important."

"Send him in, Barb. May as well tell everyone to go back to work. I'll get to them as soon as possible."

"Yessir." She departed Ed's inner office.

Sheriff Townsend was angry. "Where do you get off tellin' my men to do drug investigations?" he blurted as he stormed into Ed's office.

"That son of a bitch."

"What son of a bitch?"

"Moss. Betcha he told you that."

"Yeah, he did."

"You oughtta fire that bastard, Mike. He's playin' us off against each other. You don't need trouble like that."

Realizing he'd been had, Townsend picked up the phone and dialed his office, demanding Moss report upstairs.

"Oh he's working an accident, Sheriff," his dispatcher reported.

"Uh huh…10-20?"

"County Road and Saylor."

"C'mon, Ed." Townsend grabbed his hat and led the charge downstairs to his car. "That son of a bitch." He turned on the emergency lights, but no siren as he sped out of the courthouse parking lot.

"He's gonna get you in big trouble some day, Mike. You really oughtta can his ass."

"He brings home the state marksmanship trophy every year, Ed. Kinda puts us on the map."

"He'll put you on the map all right."

Some fifteen minutes later they drove up on the deserted intersection. Now Townsend was really livid. Where could that bastard be?

"Try the café in Drakesburg."

Drakesburg was a very small village out in the county, with only a gas station, general store, café and grain elevator to its name.

"Sure enough. How do you know this shit, Ed?"

"Wish I was wrong this time….look at the car two down from his unit."

"Oh God."

"This guy is gonna get the pants sued off you some day, Mike."

"I'll break this little party up right now." He reached for the door handle and started to get out.

"Better not, Mike."

"Why not?"

"Because these FBI bastards might just be desperate enough to retaliate. I heard Moss talkin' about a reverse sting."

Townsend slapped his hand to his forehead. "What is this son of a bitch tryin' to *do* to me."

"C'mon, Mike, we better get back to the courthouse before we're spotted."

. . . .

You could cut the tension inside the office with a knife as the two men in business suits accompanied Moss and his very angry boss.

Everyone sat at the conference table.

"Boy have we got a deal for you, Mister Cranford!" the FBI man introduced as DeWitt spoke up.

"I'm sure you do," Cranford responded glumly. "The usual federal crap."

"Your man Moss here obviously is innovative," the FBI man introduced as Smallwood added.

Cranford laughed, drawing hard stares from the federal agents. He turned to Townsend. "You even wanna *hear* this, Sheriff?"

Townsend shrugged.

"Basically, we have a pound of diluted cocaine and two first rate undercover people…one sells to the local pusher, the other buys from him."

"Oh yeah, the entrapment ploy…real smart whichever agent you are."

Mike Townsend laughed. Cranford *could not* tell FBI agents apart.

"Let me see the records of these first rate undercover people."

"Sorry, that's confidential."

"Very well. Good day, gentlemen. We don't play that way here."

"You can't demand the records of a federal informant." DeWitt smugly spoke.

Cranford reached for the phone and dialed.

"Paula Winters, please."

The two FBI men stiffened upon hearing the name.

"Hello Paula! Say are you prosecuting a reverse sting using the child molester and the rapist as undercover people?"

"Wouldn't be caught dead with it, huh? Me neither. Oh he is…. Thanks for the info. Yeah later." Cranford snickered as he hung up the phone.

He fixed a look of disgust on the FBI men. "She said the rapist is actually a sodomizer. My mistake."

"How did you know?"

"Because those are the people you always break out of state prisons and use for your crap."

"It doesn't matter….they'll never find out."

"The hell they won't. Our discovery laws require disclosure of stuff like that."

"That's okay, we have a phony rap sheet for each of them."

Cranford drilled a look of anger into Moss. "You were gonna lie to a state judge Moss?"

"The federal government said it was okay."

"And I say it's NOT okay. What are you gonna do about this Mike?"

"Moss, you are suspended for two weeks, starting now. Surrender your badge and weapon to your sergeant downstairs. That's all."

The infuriated deputy stood up and stormed out of the office, the FBI men right behind.

"I gotta wash my hands after dealing with those scum."

"Are they all that bad?"

"Pretty much, Mike. Any time you see an FBI man telling you about these great cases you get to take to court, you can bet the farm the US Attorney has already turned it down, or it was a careless slip-shod piece of trash thrown together for state scum, to pump up their statistics."

"Damn."

"Yeah…. it's kinda scary about Moss too. I wouldn't take anything of his for quite awhile, Mike."

"He's fired. As of this minute."

"Good for you."

The intercom buzzed. "Yes, Barb?"

"They're ready."

"Okay. Mike I have to get this staff meeting out of the way. You're welcome to stay if you want."

"Thanks, Ed, but I wanna get that termination paperwork pro-cessed TOOOOday!"

"I'm all for that. See ya, Mike."

. . . .

"The biggest problem at the moment is we are one attorney down… the deputy position. Marian, do you have our ad submitted yet?"

"Yessir. To the Bar Bulletin as well as the State's Attorneys' Asso-ciation flyer."

"Don't you think I should have first crack at that?" Paul Feingold spoke up.

"You're the acting," Cranford replied. "Problem is you have to be able to succeed me indefinitely and you don't have your five in yet."

"That law stinks."

"Well, you know how to change it. I think we'll use the same traffic management system Gil used. I'll take the cases I'm giving me off the top, then you two get together and dole out the rest. Any problems let me know. I'll want to meet with the attorneys weekly to discuss strategy, legal issues, that sort of thing. Karen, you meet with whoever you need to.

"Also....we were billed $65 last month on those damned 900 calls. I want that paid up by the end of the week and I want it stopped. If the paper ever got a hold of that it would be a major embarrassment. We are very busy in here these days. I may need to allocate a realignment of duties if anyone thinks they can handle more."

Marty Droud avoided eye contact, even as he appeared to be about ready to disappear under the table.

"One more thing, then I'll open it up. This office by law is responsible for deciding what cases get prosecuted and which do not. I happen to know that at least two people regularly give information to the city police.

"I want it stopped right now. If anyone continues to do that after today they will be terminated. Any questions?

"Okay...anybody have something they'd like to bring up?"

"Harry?"

"I'd like to remind the lawyers again that we are available to provide all kinds of investigative assistance. Louie and I between us have seventy years investigative experience."

"I thought we were to get follow-up from the cop turning in the case." Susan Toulouse reminded.

"You are," Cranford replied. "And while we're on that I'd strongly suggest to the lawyers that they make sure all crucial follow-up is done *before* you file it in Magistrate Court. Once you file it, a lazy cop has you by the...uh...he has it all his way thereafter.

"What Harry is talking about is additional investigative help."

. . . .

The meeting had been over for a couple hours when Cranford looked up to see Mike Townsend, his face white as a sheet, stumbling into his office.

"Oh *no!*"

"Yeah, Ed. Yeah. I oughtta resign right now."

"Why did you let him *do* that to you?"

"The campaign needed money. The Chief had it….I sorta fudged the report form…at his advice."

"You realize he owns you from now on?"

"Could you take another look at that case?"

"You really want three foul balls as Moss and those feds letting a whole pound of coke walk in our county?"

"Of course I don't Ed…. But they *are* first rate undercovers."

"Really? A child molester and a sodomizer? Listen, Mike, the first thing you need to know about the FBI is they don't give a damn about our neighborhoods or anyone else's. All they care about is their damn statistics. In fact they bring cases like this right to us because they think they can cut corners… get even more statistics."

The Sheriff of Garfield County buried his head dejectedly in his hands. "I'm finished, Ed. All washed up." He wobbled dejectedly to his feet, unpinned his badge, dropped it on Cranford's desk and stumbled out.

As rare as gunshots fired within the walls of the courthouse were, this one was somehow no surprise to Cranford. For a man like Townsend it was really the only way open to him. The State's Attorney had now buried seven friends in this filthy business.

Seven… and the number would no doubt keep rising.

He put on his topcoat as he reached the back lot and headed for the black Ford.

January 3, 1981: The Cranford home.

The drive home passed in a daze. The radio was full of traffic calling for ambulances, the city's forensics team, crime scene experts.

"Somebody murdered himself at your work, Dad." Eleven year old Chris spoke as soon as Ed was through the door.

"I know, son, I heard the shot."

"Did you see any blood?"

"Not this time."

"Okay if I tell Denny you saw blood?"

"I see enough of it, that's for sure."

"Oh boy! I'm gonna tell him right now!" Chris went charging out the front door about two seconds ahead of Gwenn yelling at him to get ready for dinner.

"Are you gonna have to be gone all night, Daddy?" Nine year old Lupe asked.

"Maybe, sweetie, we'll know pretty soon."

The phone in the kitchen began ringing.

"Shit! That's probably them calling now."

"You get it," Gwenn snapped. "I have better things to do than be your secretary."

"What's for dinner?" Ed asked.

"There's the oven, go look for yourself."

Ed picked up the phone and said hello.

It was Harding Carraway, editor of the *Ojo Urioste*. The Chief *hated* Carraway. Carraway for some reason liked Cranford. "You got a comment, Ed?"

"The death of Sheriff Mike Townsend is a great personal loss and a great loss to the people of Garfield County."

"Great comment, Ed. Is the sheriff dead too?"

"Huh? You mean he isn't?"

"No....Dave Moss, a deputy."

"*Seriously?*"

"What made you think it was Mike?"

"Ohhhhh...everybody."

"*Everybody?*"

"Sorry, Harding. It's been that kind of a day."

"It's only your first... as top gun."

"Ohhhh don't remind me."

Carraway laughed. "Seriously Cranford, what made you think it was Mike?"

Cranford had already said way too much…maybe already enough to get his friend in serious trouble. "It's his office, I just naturally thought of him first. Glad it wasn't though."

"I can't imagine anyone would want to murder Mike."

"*Murder?*"

"*You don't think so?*"

"Now that you say it was Moss, I wouldn't rule out accidental discharge."

"What makes you say that?"

"The man was careless. Hey I better ring off, Harding. They may be callin' me down there later."

"Better you than me, Ed. Later!"

"Bye Harding."

Cranford hung up the phone now very worried about Mike. Dialing his unlisted home number, he got the Sheriff on the third ring.

"How are you, Mike? You've had me pretty scared."

"That makes two of us. Oh Ed I…."

"Hold it, Mike… don't tell me anything. And don't tell any cops anything."

"You sure that's wise?"

"I'm positive, Mike. Listen, I'm gonna call some ace lawyers I know. If I can get one to see you will you talk to him?"

"Yeah….if you think I should."

"Yes, I do…but above all I don't want you to make any statements to any cops."

"Okay, Ed. Just call me back quick. I'm awful scared."

"I will. Just hang on." Cranford hung up the phone, then went into his and Gwenn's bedroom. Picking up a black memo book, he leafed through it.

His first choice didn't answer. His second was busy. He got through to his third.

"How's your caseload these days, Lisa?"

"Picking up smartly, Ed."

"Well great. Could you take on one more at this point?:

"Degree of difficulty?"

"Moderate. Could be murder….*very* high profile if it is.

"You intrigue me, sweetie."

"Think you could get out here tonight? He's really scared."

"You don't ask much, do you? Awww, Ed, that's *two hundred miles.*"

"Maybe I could send him to you."

"Check that out, Ed. It would be much better for me."

"I will. Sit tight."

The bottom line was that Mike Townsend would gladly drive two hundred miles if Lisa Rockwell could make him less afraid. Ed thought she could. By midnight she called him to say Mike had made it safely. Then came the zinger.

"How bad does it look Lisa?"

"He swears he didn't have his gun all day, that it was in his desk. Can you help with any of that?"

"He didn't have it the hour or so during the day he was with me. He never carries it on him when he's in the office."

"He says that when he went from your office back to his own he looked for it….it was missing from his desk drawer."

Suddenly the whole awful mess was taking shape. Moss would be found to have been shot with Mike's gun…Mike would get the blame. He told Lisa.

"What did you say the degree of difficulty was?"

"Just went up a few notches didn't it?"

He no sooner hung up than his doorbell rang. Answering it, he beheld the cruelest, most brutal cop in Garfield County… Fritz Strachmann.

"Where's Townsend, Cranford?"

"Well he's not here if that's what you think."

"Mind if I look around?"

"Sorry….just put the kids down."

"I could get a warrant and tear this place apart."

Cranford laughed. "Grow up, Strachmann. But if you wanna give me a nice big retirement bonus, go for it."

"You're up to your ears in this thing, Pantywaist. But if you want to dick around, two can play that game." With that he slammed Cranford's front door, then shortly afterward was heard peeling out in his police car.

With shaking hands, the State's Attorney turned out the lights, then joined Gwenn in bed.

"So who do you represent? The criminals or the cops?"

"The criminals, Gwenn."

"Takes one to know one."

"Must be why I get them all off."

"I don't like it here."

"Me neither."

"Well then why do we have to stay here?"

"Because it's the only job I have right now."

"Maybe Roberto can find you one."

"He's welcome to try."

"Really? I'll tell mom tomorrow we're moving back."

"You do that, Gwenn."

Thursday January 6, 1981: Division I courtroom; Garfield County Courthouse

Cranford slipped into the back of the courtroom. Judge Santestevan saw him and gave the faintest of nods. The judge had told him he really needed to come see Susan Toulouse in action. At issue was a defense motion to suppress evidence. It was a dope case…a vehicle search growing out of a traffic stop.

So far the defense attorney had his prosecutor thrashing around trying to say that since the defendant could grab the keys from the cop at any minute, despite being handcuffed, that exigent circumstances existed in fact throughout the stop. Cranford winced not believing what he was hearing.

As unobtrusively as possible, Cranford made the 'time-out' sign with his hands. Santestevan kept the hearing going another four minutes, then interrupted the defense attorney in the middle of a witness. I'm sorry Mister Terry, Ms Toulouse…the Court has a brief telephonic hearing in chambers. We will be in recess for twenty minutes. With that he left the courtroom.

Susan caught sight of the boss. "Doing pretty good don't you think?"

"You don't need to prove exigency in fact, Susan. It's presumed in a vehicle stop."

"Oh I knew that. I was just showing that bastard we have proof to spare."

Unfortunately, Susan had the failing common to those for whom law was way over their heads. She knew it all.

Cranford headed for the office. He needed Marian to advertise for two lawyers.

He had no sooner given her the message when Strachmann walked in.

"Where are you hidin' him, Cranford?"

"Who, Fritz?"

Strachmann rolled his eyes.

"Can't find him, huh?"

"We'll find him… don't you worry about that."

"Well in that case I can go back to work." Cranford started down the corridor to his office.

"You ever hear of accessory charges?"

"Noooooo. Just one more example of how brilliant you are."

His next comment was drowned out by Cranford slamming his door. He heard some whispering between Droud and Strachmann.

As soon as Urioste's pet boy left, he called Marty in.

"I guess you didn't take my hint."

"About what, sir?"

"Don't insult my intelligence, Marty. Did you pay the 900 phone bill yet?"

"To the penny."

The smug smile disappeared when Cranford got Marian on the line. "Not a penny," was her comment.

"Come on…let's get your appointment book." Cranford leafed through it. "You don't have a single appointment this entire week. What the hell do you do around here, Marty?"

"First of the year is always slow."

B ring me all your files, Marty, right now."

He was back in five minutes with an armload of thick files.

"Now…careful, Marty. I've caught you in one lie already. One more and you start feeling my outrage. How many of these are *current, active* people you are supervising?"

He took maybe five files off the pile.

"Did you understand my question?"

"Yes sir!"

"What did I ask?"

"You asked me for the files of my current active cases."

"What is that pile of files there?"

"My current active files. They all really like you by the way, Mister Cran…"

"Last chance, Marty.…what is that pile?"

"My current active."

Cranford took a file from the middle and opened it. "Mid December you saw this guy last. Are these appointment times accurate?"

"To the minute."

Cranford picked up the phone and dialed an intercom . "Marian, bring me that pile of 900 calls please."

She brought the stack. Cranford looked through them.

"According to this, you were on the 900 boxing line for a whole hour during the time this guy was supposedly with you."

He slammed the file folder to the table. "You really insult my intelligence putting me through this, damn you."

"Oh I remember! That was the day my watch stopped."

"That day and all the rest.

"Okay…. Tomorrow you will take yourself to the capital and go to the State's Attorney's Office. You will spend the next five working days doing OJT with their probation officer. You will not make a single phone call nor put a drop of gas in the car. You have just enough.

"I want you at the office eight hours a day, five days a week. Understood?"

"Yessir."

"The slightest deviation from these instructions and…."

"I'm fired."

"When you come back we'll see how you do. That's all."

He picked up the files and left.

Cranford dialed the intercom. "Harry, come in here please."

The chief investigator came in.

"Think you can tail Marty up in the capital for a week without him knowing?"

"Sure."

"Okay.... Get his complete motel bill, also the complete report of expenditure on the state credit card. Also I want a candid appraisal from his opposite number up there... how he did in the OJT."

"Marty's a foul ball."

"Yes he is."

Chambers of the Hon. Gilbert Maynard Beecham

"So that was like the third lie I'd caught him in."

Beecham laughed.

"How could you *hire* talent like that?"

"The Chief told me he needed a job."

"So he just dumped him on you."

Beecham gave one of his sly smiles. "It wasn't entirely a one way street. He saw to it the Chief was well pleased with my cooperation, all the while thinking he was outwitting me."

"I've sent him for a week of OJT. If he violates one of the condition s he's fired."

Beecham angrily shook his head. "And you'll be fired within thirty days."

"And of course Marty knows this."

"Marty knows this."

"Cranford you are a born politician, but your suicidal bullshit will prevent you from ever succeeding. Keep your car locked, check your bank account every fifteen days..."

"So Sheriff DeLuca was right."

"Yes, he was right."

Cranford knew Beecham was reading his '*how could you*' look.

"I'm not the least bit ashamed, Ed. The people of Garfield County got one hell of a State's Attorney. The price was small, just a few dummies who didn't know enough to come in out of the rain. I insisted they be warned. They didn't take the warning."

"Is this my warning?"

"No. You'll be told what you've done wrong and given the chance to correct it."

Cranford stood up. "Well thanks for your time, Judge."

"Not at all. How are things with Gwenn?"

"They suck."

Beecham shook his head. "Get her out of here before she collapses on your flank."

"Meaning what?"

"Meaning things so awful I cannot describe them for you."

"My God. Tell me who in real life would want to work 15 hour days in the cause of law enforcement just to have the cops destroy you?"

"There's a riddle for you. Good bye, Cranford."

"Wait a minute, Gil… why *are* the best prosecutors brought down by cops?"

Beecham gave his suddenly unwelcome visitor a look of disgust. "You still have a lot to learn don't you?"

"I'd like to learn that right now if you don't mind."

"Okay, Ed, say you've got a really good prosecutor… and say he ramrods an investigation that takes the twenty people who supply drugs by the ton to all the other millions of pushers down to the smallest user… now I'm just using the figure of twenty hypothetically. But say there are only twenty at the very pinnacle…and say this brilliant prosecutor takes them all out.

"Are the cops happy or sad?"

"Happy. They cleaned up the town."

"Let me put it another way. Remember when you were doing all those forfeitures for the Highway Patrol?"

"Don't remind me."

"Ah HAH! What happened, Cranford?"

"The top brass started picking the targets, not based on sound narcotics enforcement, but because they wanted a particular car to drive."

"And how many of those cars were actually used in drug enforcement?"

"Only the pimpmobiles. The rest all went to guys that hadn't been on the street in years. Bigshots."

"Uh huh. What else?"

"The *Capital City Register* did a big write up on all the millions of dollars we had seized. In response to this information, the General Assembly cut our budget by a couple million, saying we could get the rest in forfeitures."

"So the forfeiture demon took on a life of its own, didn't it?"

"It became something we *had* to do to stay afloat."

"Not at all what was originally intended by the law, was it?"

"No, it became utter venality...greed. The drug enforcement kind of got lost in the shuffle."

"Yeah....do you also remember the day all these weird federal guys with coke bottle glasses descended on your headquarters, asking questions?"

"Yes, they wanted to learn what our guys on the highway were doing to bag all those drugs."

"Did you tell 'em?"

"The bosses did. The Highway Patrol was encouraged to apply for several million in federal grants, to better fund the enforcement effort."

"Yeah...now the $64,000 question, Cranford.... In the three years you've been gone, how many large amounts of drugs have been seized on the highway by your old agency?"

Cranford shook his head in disbelief. "I don't think they've done any, Gil."

"I agree.... Do you think the feds tipped the major suppliers off?"

"The feds are royal fuckups, but I'd hate to believe that."

"Well in actual fact it doesn't matter. Three years after the feds came and essentially began shutting down the most effective state enforcement program in the country, your old agency can no longer afford to do major seizures."

"I don't follow."

"It's very simple. With the coming of the federal grants the Highway Patrol got fancy new police cars, really cool assault rifles, terrific body armor, state of the art night vision scopes and no less than twenty new positions...."

"Only problem is, to keep all those positions and get more fancy toys they have to make a lot of arrests. That's how the feds administer those grants…they wanna see lotsa druggies arrested….the state has to report the number of drug arrests each year and it has to be high."

"Bloody hell."

"I can see you're learning Cranford. Now all the Highway Patrol can afford to get is one rock crack dealers, quarter ounce pot sellers. You can round up fifty of those guys with one sting op. Of course their replacements are on the street that afternoon, but the cops could care less. They are guaranteeing their jobs for another year.

"The so-called War on Drugs is the worst thing that's ever happened to this country. It thrives on the continuation of the drug problem…it feeds on the guaranteed failure of enforcement efforts. It virtually guarantees the immunity of the truly big time dealer because to take him out would dry up his whole supply chain of some two to three hundred people. And that's only one lousy arrest."

"Wow."

"Bottom line, one mediocre prosecutor who follows orders is all that's required. There are hate crime grants, sex crime grants, white collar crime grants. All of these demand the guaranteed increase in arrests year after year."

"You're a bundle of joy today, Gil."

"Keep smilin', Ed. And for God's sake follow orders. Believe me you won't be missed. The day they bury you crime will be thriving just like always. The cops will see to that. They want to keep their jobs. Can't really blame 'em."

"I worked with the best at CIB….Now I'm depressed."

"It's not worth it, Ed. None of it's worth it."

. . . .

Cranford dragged himself home, went into the bedroom and stretched out on the queen size mattress. Gwenn had the news on, the anchorman blabbing about some boat overturning, costing over two hundred people their lives.

Cranford wondered if any of those poor souls were in the fix he was. He wondered if any of them saw the rising waters as deliverance. He went back to his earlier riddle wondering why he'd burned a hole clear through his stomach lining working fifteen hour days so those same cops could someday destroy him when he became too unreliable.

He swallowed two 500mg Tylenols with a Pepsi. Gwenn appeared at the door. "Mom wants to know exactly when we're moving back."

"Day after tomorrow."

Gwenn looked at him incredulously. "Really?"

"Saturday at the latest."

"WOW!" She went running off to call her mom.

He closed his eyes. Fire Marty and I've got thirty days. Don't fire Marty and I lose control of the office.

It was the end of his fourth full day. The vultures were starting to gather on the telephone wires. Marty, Strachmann, Paul Feingold, still enraged he wasn't the new Deputy, no doubt those two FBI bastards.

Four days....five vultures. Obviously those wires would soon be *very* crowded.

Chapter Three

You Can't Keep a Good Man Dead

Friday January 14, 1981: the Cranford home.

Ed got his coffee and Gwenn's from the kitchen. Handing her cup into her, he got back into bed, lit a Chesterfield and started sipping.

"I'm really angry you lied to me about when we were moving. You really embarrassed me in front of my mom."

"I doubt your mom…."

"You lied to me, Ed. You're such a liar."

"That'll teach you next time, Gwenn."

"Teach me what?"

"Not to believe me."

Gwenn exhaled sharply. "Sure wish I hadn't quit smoking. I really need one today."

Ed held out the pack. She took one and lit up.

"Ohhhh, that's sooooo good."

"I don't know how you are able to quit like you do."

"I was pregnant. My baby's health was more important than my desire to sin."

"Hmmmm. That's me…the Ol' Sinner."

"The Old Liar you mean."

"That too."

"So all right. When are we moving?"

"Just as soon as I can line up a job in the capital."

"Have you even tried?"

"The AG so far."

"Nothing else?"

"So far, no. I had one of my investigators up there this week. He was supposed to pick up a few applications for me."

"I want to get out of here just as soon as possible."

"Me too, Gwenn."

"I wish I could believe that."

"I wish you could too. Then you wouldn't have to worry so much."

"Just stop lying all the time."

Ed glanced at the clock radio. "Shit! I better get down there."

"Just stop lying."

"Yeah….I'll have to work on that."

The hard freeze the past night made scraping the windscreen take at least 15 minutes. There was still close to six inches of snow on the ground and the dark gray skies seemed to say there might be a bunch more by sundown.

The road was covered with ice as he headed for All Wars and a nicely sanded drive all the way downtown.

A block and a half away and Ed was in trouble. A giant Grand Marquis came sliding around the corner, wildly fishtailing. He brought the state car to an easy stop but the heavy vehicle plowed into him, causing his vehicle to spin 180 degrees.

"You hurt, lady?" Ed panted as he got out of the car, hands shaking.

"This is fine snow clearance. I could have been killed. You know you should allow space for skidding vehicles."

"I'm a liar too. Are you hurt?"

"Fortunately for you, no."

Ed reached in and pulled the radio mike out. "801 city, over."

"Go ahead 801."

"Involved in 10-44 Conley and Wright."

When the woman saw the radio mike, her eyes then darted to the official plates. "Oh my God… what rotten luck…a cop."

"How do you know it's a 44, 801?"

"Woman says so."

"10-4, sir. We'll roll a 10-55 just to be safe."

"10-4… lemme have a 28, 29 in-state plate Nora Edward Paul 479 displayed on a 1980 dark green Grand Marquis."

"10-4….10-23."

"Oh you won't arrest me will you officer?"

"I'm the State's Attorney, ma'am. The city police are coming."

"Headquarters 801."

"Go ahead."

"Are you 10-12?" Ed tensed. That was only asked when something bad was coming up, for the officer's protection. Ed moved inside the car and closed the door.

"Negative, city."

"License returns on a 1974 Mustang. The car you have was reported stolen after woman requested a test drive. Woman is escaped mental patient. May be armed. 10-80."

This day is off to a great start. He depressed the mike button. "I'll do what I can, but the woman appears easily agitated."

"10-4, 801. She takes anti-psychotic medication. Hasn't had a dose in three days. Repeat, 10-48 possible… 10-80."

"801…out." Ed took a deep breath and again got out of the car. "They'll be here any minute, ma'am."

"Well I have a body in the trunk which deserves Christian burial and I was on the way to the cemetery again to do that when you failed to leave enough room for skidding cars."

"If we put some ice cubes on the body it will be all right."

"That's *right*! I can see you're a very smart young man. I'll go get some right now."

"Actually it's against the law to leave the scene of an accident, ma'am."

"Yes, but you see I killed the poor man in the trunk, so it's really kind of silly doing the space cadet routine."

"I can see your point, ma'am." Off in the distance but coming his way on foot, Ed could see a young woman. *Where in hell is that cop?*

"So not wishing to be the tail end of the rainbow, I will shake up the ice cube situation."

"That'll just result in margaritas. You'd best leave the ice cubes to me."

"You're pretty smart, young man. I completely overlooked our sheriff."

"*What?*"

"It was the middle of the night. The poor man appeared entirely pixilated. I knew he wasn't happy. In fact he was dead!"

The young woman looked familiar, but Ed couldn't place her. She was now just a few feet away. When he turned his attention back to the woman, however, she was pointing a magnum revolver at him.

"You look very pixilated and unhappy."

"Right on both counts, lady, but there's no room for me in the trunk."

"Oh I pack very well." She pulled the hammer back, then let out a screech as the young woman gave her a chop to the neck. The revolver clattered to the street as Ed stepped on it.

The woman let out a bloodcurdling shriek as she lunged for the leg Ed had positioned on the revolver. The young woman delivered a roundhouse kick to the head, causing the older woman to flatten herself on the ice, then go limp.

"Good morning, Mr. Cranford."

"Good morning angel of mercy. Much obliged by the way."

She smiled. "It's kind of a different feeling being on this side of the law."

With that remark he snapped. This was Kelly Miksis. While her own legal problems seemed confined to misdemeanor drug abuse, she was in the photo album of every drug pusher in town. As camera technology was starting to cut out the necessity for taking film to be developed, more local losers were photographing themselves and their girlfriends naked. It was in these photo spreads one could always find Kelly.

In Ed's experience, most druggie girlfriends were fat with orange hair. In this crowd Kelly was a standout. She had a nice figure, long black hair, large dark eyes and the olive complexion often associated with Greco-Americans. The problem was she probably had every kind of VD known to man, given the company she kept.

"What are you doing walking around on such a bitter cold morning….besides saving my life that is?"

"They lifted my license, Mr. Cranford, and I have to meet with my probation officer today."

"So you're going to the courthouse?"

"Yessir."

"I'll gladly give you a lift…if you don't mind being seen in such company."

"Thank …oh wait." She delivered a fast kick to the woman's wrist, sending a .380 automatic sliding along the ice as the woman once more let out a blood-curdling shriek.

"Damn… I'm just not thinking this morning. Could you search this character for me, Kelly? I'll witness it so nobody can try to set you up."

"Sure, but keep a close eye. Strachmann has said he's gonna frame me some day."

"*Really*? He talks to you like that?"

"If you'll pardon my French, Mr. Cranford, he's the person the word 'pig' was made for."

Ed nodded, disgusted but not at all surprised.

The search revealed a man's wallet with all ID removed. Only the stub of a bus ticket remained, dated two days ago from the state capital. The leather was well worn, but the initials' DM' could be seen along the front.

At long last, Officer Danny Steele drove up with a well dressed man in the passenger seat.

"What took you so long, Danny?"

"I had to pick up Mr. Becker. He wanted the car returned right away."

"When somebody's out by himself with a mental patient, you get there ASAP. Didn't you know that?"

"Deputy Chief Strachmann's orders."

Becker had already grabbed the keys from the woman's pocket after Steele handcuffed her. He was making for the car.

"Just a second, Mister Becker," Cranford called out. "Steele, you better open the trunk first before you contaminate a potential crime scene."

"I'm in a hurry, whoever you are." Becker pulled out a laminated card stating he was a member of the 'Hank Urioste 100 Grand Club'.

He was one of the ten or so citizens who donated a hundred grand to the police chief's war chest. In return these men got anything they wanted… or so it was rumored.

"Steele, before you make what may turn out to be a very serious mistake, take a look at the big stain on the passenger floorboard, then this wallet. This woman told me she had a body in there."

Becker was indignant. "Listen Sonny, I'll have you pounding a beat at Five Points. I'm a very busy man. Steele, you'll be with him."

"Take it Mister Becker. I apologize."

The angry fat cat roared off in a dense cloud of hydrocarbon pollution.

"Sorry, Mister Cranford."

"Not half as sorry as you will be if there is a body in there. And I'll tell you, you leave any officer alone with a violent mental patient and you are looking at personal liability.

"But Strachmann said…"

"That just means they'll have two fools to laugh at instead of one. C'mon Kelly."

They were both quiet most of the way in.

"Gee, Mister Cranford, the cops are just as nasty to you as they are to us," Kelly finally spoke as the black Ford pulled into the courthouse parking lot.

"Mercifully this town is an unusual exception."

"I'm glad to hear that."

"By the way, if you need a ride home, come up to the office when you're done. It's the least I can do for you."

"Thanks, Mister Cranford…. See you later then." She flashed a dazzling smile as Ed watched her disappear through the back door of the courthouse.

Dragging himself up to the third floor, Ed had Harry Kinney come to his office. He came in with several sheets of paper and an investigator's notebook.

"I'll give you the compliance part first, Chief. He went to the capital, he went to the State's Attorney's Office. He even stayed a half hour."

"That's all?"

"Yes. The rest of the week he watched ESPN, ran up an $85 phone bill on 900 sports line calls and talked a couple times to Urioste in excess of thirty minutes. He filled the tank of the state car twice while there, and parked it in the lot of a notorious sports bar all day every day while he was inside getting tanked, again all on the state credit card."

"Obviously the chief told him not to worry."

"Yes. What's gonna happen, Boss?"

"He's O-U-T."

"How long do you think he'll stay gone?"

"Until the Chief tells the Governor who to appoint to take my place."

The chief investigator appeared sad as he looked down. "So you're really cashin' in, huh?"

"There is no way I could let that lazy con man run this office… no way. Tell him to step in on the way back to your office, Harry."

"Okay, Boss." He shook his head sadly. "Sorry you're going." Without another word he was through the door.

Marty Droud came in less than a minute later. "They really respect you up in the cap…"

"How did you do on the OJT?"

"Great!"

"How many tanks of gas did you put in?"

"Not a drop."

"How many phone calls did you make?"

"Not a one! You told me not to."

"Have a seat, Marty."

"I don't know who Urioste has in mind to succeed me, but I'm sure that person will give you your job back."

His eyes widened.

"Some people actually believe that quality workmanship is less important than loyalty. In that arena, you score every time. Since this isn't *LEAVE IT TO BEAVER* there is no lesson to be learned, but maybe someday you will learn of the pride that accompanies a job well done. If that happens you will learn at last what we have been trying to tell you."

"Effective forthwith you are terminated, Marty.... For dishonesty, embezzlement, nonfeasance in office. We are attaching your last paycheck as restitution for the embezzlement. Agree with that or we'll prosecute.

"Although you will be back in less than a month, you still need to remove your things from your office. I'm giving it to Louie Gabaldón."

That last revelation had Marty looking gutshot. The old bastard was giving his office to the only other spy.

"Louie is also taking the probation officer position. I need that program to run successfully. Louie is a hard worker.

"That's all, Marty."

He had hoped to revel in his early return, but the old bastard was going to make it a lot more difficult than either he or Urioste had planned. He literally stumbled out the door.

An hour later, Cranford had the newspaper, radio and television reporters in his office, eagerly snapping pictures of and recording his presentation.

"The 900 sports toll calls now top over $100...and this is just within this past month. These records tell us Droud spent hours every week running up the state's phone bill, money he was fully expecting you the people of Garfield County to pay for. These hours were spent listening to rundowns of past football games and prognostications of the coming weekend, as well as similar stuff about boxing.

"Additionally we have eyewitness accounts he spent most of last week that I scheduled him for remedial training in a sports bar, drinking on a state credit card, driving to and from in a state car.

"The bottom line is he chose to ignore direct warnings about his dishonesty and efforts to give him remedial training. He also continually refused to pay the state back for those phone calls. I have therefore this day terminated him, and given his duties to Louie Gabaldón, who until now was an investigator with us. Louie is an honest man and a hard worker who will drive us where we want to go with the probation officer position.

"I'll take a couple questions....Yes, Harding."

"Last year Droud was identified as a major force in Chief Urioste's lobbying organization. It was rumored the Chief pretty much told

Beecham to give him a job. Being that no one here was born yes-terday, can you tell us anything about your longevity in light of this termination?"

"I'm finished."

Several shocked expressions were looking back at the State's Attorney.

"I hope no one had to grow up too quickly." Scattered chuckles were heard around the room.

"Mind you there are other factors besides. Fritz Strachmann told the officer coming to back me up to deliberately wait, leaving me to handle an escaped mental patient alone, contrary to the policy of every law enforcement agency I'm aware of. I just had a new baby daughter….neither my wife nor I need this kind of treatment."

"Jill…"

"When do you actually plan to vacate?"

"The very minute I get a job at the capital…. At the latest."

"Who do you plan to recommend for your replacement?"

"Obviously we need a man with the patience and tact of a Gil Beecham. Since I know of no such person, I will simply suggest the Governor hear the recommendation of Chief Urioste."

"Why would you do that?" an astonished Harding Carraway asked.

"One of the wisest men I know told me recently that the best thing for Garfield County is…and this is an exact quote… a mediocre pros-ecutor that follows orders."

Now it was a sea of shocked faces looking back at Cranford.

"If you don't like what such a quote appears to say about your home, how do you think I saw it as a comment on my job?"

There were a lot of shaking heads and frowns.

"Dennis?"

"I for one have been completely in the dark about the apparent bar-rage of discouragement you've gotten here, Ed. Is there anything we can do to make it a bit more encouraging for you?"

"To be honest, Dennis, you folks already are my encouragement. When all is said and done working for these cops….working yourself into an early grave just to have them leave you without backup first chance they get…will cancel out the efforts of people with the real interest of this community at heart. It is truly unfortunate, but please believe I will remember all of you quite warmly however long or short the rest of my career is fated to be."

It was a glum group that filed out of Ed's office an hour or so after they'd first come in.

In the final thirty minutes of the day he called his staff into his office. All except Marty who by then was gone.

"I won't keep you…. This won't take long. Firstly, Louie… you will be our new probation officer beginning Monday. You should move into the office reserved for that position by Monday noon if at all possible. Think you'll be able to?"

"No problem, boss."

"Okay…. The other bit of news is I am sending my resignation to the Governor."

The reaction was mainly one of shock.

"But you *can't!*" Barbara blurted.

"I'll just save our police chief some time. I terminated Marty today. Everyone has been telling me it would mean my doom. Frankly though, I am so tired of having to look upon cops as my enemy that the job, my whole career path, just makes no sense anymore."

"If anybody needed terminating it was that little con man," Marian spat.

Karen, Barb, Harry and Vickie all nodded agreement.

"The first thing you learn about dirty politics is those are the kind of people they protect. The good ones don't need it." Ed looked at his watch.

"Okay, that's …"

"How much longer will you stay?" Barb asked.

"Not sure. But I certainly won't keep my successor waiting for his office."

"Who is your successor going to be?"

"No idea, Karen. I'll let you know what I know as soon as I know it. Okay, let's go home.

"Paul you've got a trial Monday, so you'll have my full attention this weekend if you want it."

He nodded.

With that, a very confused and troubled group put covers on type-writers, loaded briefcases with weekend work and then departed. Ed made straight for the black Ford. Kelly was standing beside it.

"I wondered what happened to you. Were you with your P.O. all day?"

She laughed. "No, I just decided to spend some time downtown."

Ed opened her door and she climbed in, reaching over and unlocking his.

For once, Ed turned off the police radio and turned on the 5pm news.

At the top of the news this hour, State's Attorney Edward A. Cranford dropped a bombshell at a hastily called press conference by announcing he was resigning his office and would be returning to the state capital where his wife is from. Cranford cited interagency disharmony and failing health as two of the reasons supporting his decision.

Earlier Cranford reviewed with reporters the decision to terminate 24 year old Marty Droud, who worked with the office as a probation officer. Droud was terminated for dishonesty and embezzlement. He is a reputed close friend of Police Chief Enrique Urioste Seguín.

Cranford reached over and switched the radio off. "No peace no matter *where* I go."

"I'm sorry to hear this Mister Cranford."

"You saw some of the main reasons for it today, Kelly."

"Yeah…I sure don't blame you, but we will miss you."

"Who do you mean?"

"Oh, just about everyone I know. You're the enemy of course, but the nice thing about you is you're not all mad dog. You treat all people with respect… a lot of us have never known that."

"Well thank you, Kelly. That means more to me than I can tell you. And I'll tell you honestly, I'd really like to help you get on another road. No pressure, in fact I promise I'll never mention it again. But if you ever wanna think about it, remember I'm here."

"But not for long."

"You'll know where I am." Cranford pulled up at a place around the block from where Kelly lived. She didn't want her roommates to see.

"Thanks again, Mister Cranford."

"Thank *you*, Kelly, for saving my worthless skin."

"I sure don't think that."

He watched until she disappeared around the corner, then drove the rest of the way home. It hadn't snowed at all today, like it was supposed to. Maybe tonight, the weather people were now saying.

When he rounded the corner to his house, Cranford did a double take. The 'Municipal Government' official plate said it all:

CITY POLICE

1

Chapter Four

Delay Is Always an Option

Friday January 14, 1981: the Cranford home

In the time it took Ed to park his car, turn off the ignition and get out, the snow began falling…hard.

Ed had always loved snow. As a young man he even used to get the "Christmas Spirit." A spirit ten times as strong when it snowed. He remembered the magical white Christmas his first year out of the service. He had chosen this state because he got out determined to marry Gwenn. He even settled in the capital. That Christmas he had showered Gwenn, Chris and Lupe with presents. He adored seeing Gwen try on the pant suits he bought her. *Gawd she was gorgeous!* For Ed's money she still was the Perfect Hispanic Beauty…rich black hair, high cheekbones and dark, dark eyes.

As the shock of seeing Urioste's car wore off, he began to wonder if he was brainwashing Gwenn. That was sure the obvious interpretation of Beecham's warning of her 'collapsing on his flank'. By the time he entered his house he was angry.

Apparently he needn't have worried. Gwenn was in the kitchen while the Chief sat on the living room couch drinking coffee. When Gwenn saw her husband she flashed a look of great relief. Gwenn was shy around strangers. In recent years she had even lost touch with her friends. Nowadays the only person she felt comfortable around was her mother.

Urioste rose when Cranford entered. "Mister State's Attorney!" he gushed, the very picture of fashion in his gray three piece pinstripe suit with blue dress shirt and burgundy tie. The trademark red carnation was in his lapel, making a striking contrast to his silver hair and Gilbert Roland matching moustache.

Ed tentatively shook the hand Urioste extended. "My apologies, sir. Here you've been our chief law enforcement officer for two weeks now and I haven't even paid a courtesy call."

"Just in the nick of time, Chief," Cranford smiled, suddenly feeling a fifty pound weight was removed from his soul. "I'll be gone before you can say 'political machine.'"

He had this reoccurring nightmare: snow was everywhere on the ground, being whipped into drifts by a merciless wind. In the dream he was always stumbling around, snow up to his knees, wearing one of his high fashion suits. In the dream Ed always saw himself at a distance… it was as if the stumbling creature had no thoughts…no sense of direction…no hope. The suits symbolized his 'optimistic period'. Here he was three years out of the service and a lawyer. He couldn't wait to get to his very own office every day.

An unbelievable achievement for a guy who started grade school mentally retarded.

But now, said the dream, all those fancy suits were good for was to provide inadequate protection from the cold…the storms of this crooked profession that consumed its dedicated members in heartless combat, buffeted them around in the grist mill of their consciences, ultimately drilling holes clear through even his once- strong Irish peasant stomach lining.

In short he was out of work, with no relief in sight.

Ed always awakened freezing and sweating at the same time. But now as he repeated his plan of imminent departure from this filthy business of trafficking in human lives, and doing a bad job of it, he felt fifty pounds lighter…free!

Earl Warren and his jackass cohorts had made a mockery of the system to begin with…making the tail wag the dog. He was a lousy lawyer so it took him and his lousy lawyer friends fifty pages to

announce a new dumb rule that had nothing to do with guilt or inno-
cence but which set a hardened criminal free.

Yes, Ed was suddenly feeling good!

"You're a card Cranford… such a card! I've heard your humor takes
no prisoners. Good for you…nothing like humor."

"Well thanks, and nice of you to come, Chief. I wanted to tell you
that if you have someone in mind to succeed me I will gladly pass it
on to the Governor on Monday."

"Truth be told, Vato, I came by to try to talk you out of such
nonsense."

Ed could feel his jaw drop. One look at his face and the Chief burst
into hysterical laughter. "Hey, Vato, you've got more friends than you
realize…and I am one of them. We *need* a man of your ethics here. To
me, you and Judge Santestevan are the slender reed holding up this
rotten modern edifice… this Earl Warren created upside world."

"Well, I don't know…"

"Jefe cuidao!" Gwenn barked as she emerged from the kitchen. Ed
and Urioste turned to face her.

"¡Queremos volver a la casa de mis padres!"

Urioste obviously hadn't considered *this* lobby. "Señora Cranford…
quienes son *nosotros* ?"

"Yo y mis hijos…los tres."

"No se preoccupe, Señora. Su esposo, sus niños y usted será bastante bien."

Gwenn appeared the picture of frustration as she saw her long
awaited move back to her mom thwarted. "Ojalá qué sí el Señor Jefe."

At times like this Ed wished Gwenn would just *butt out*. Before
she got to the part where she was divorcing Ed if he didn't agree to
leave this hellhole ASAP. He played his ace. "But Chief, I fired Marty
Droud. I wouldn't…I couldn't…take him back."

Urioste shrugged. "I don't blame you, Eddie. Marty isn't like the
others, and after all you *did* give his job to Louie." He slapped the
State's Attorney on the back, then pinched his cheek. "Shrewd move,
Eddie boy. I laughed my ass off. Know what I said?"

Cranford shook his head. "It probably wasn't very complimentary."

"The hell it wasn't, boy! I said this citified pendejo beat me at my own game! I said we need more like him."

"Then you heard the newscast."

"Yes, I heard it. Came right over."

"I don't know what to say, Chief… but I'm afraid it's not just Marty."

"Well *tell* me, boy. Quién sabe….eh?"

"Well…. This morning I was keeping an escaped mental patient at bay. I called it in, but Fritz told the backup officer to go pick up the used car dealer from whom the car was embezzled. Well the dame was armed….if it weren't for a citizen coming along, I'd be dead and that's no lie."

"He was only trying to keep good community relations,"

"You mean appeasing a member of the 100 Grand Club…."

Urioste cracked a smile.

"… at the expense of my life, Chief. I can't live…."

"Enough, boy. Enough! I'll look into it okay?"

"Please do. By the way, do I have to tell you he's a psychotic?"

"No…. But he went belly up in Korea after rescuing ten of his buddies from a Chinese assault… won the Navy Cross."

"Oh." Cranford looked hard at Urioste who seemed to be trembling. "Would one of those ten buddies be in this room?"

"By coincidence, that's so."

Now it was Cranford's turn to slap the Chief on the back. "I'll work around him, Chief. Maybe if you just brief all officers that a 10-24 takes precedence over any other orders."

Urioste was smiling as he tried to secretly wipe at his eyes. "You know, Vato, we have a saying in the Department about your office."

"I'm all ears."

"We say if you want it done fast, go to Feingold or Susan Too-loose. If you want it done right, go to Cranford."

"Did I hear that right?"

"When you ask it that way, I'd say you heard it right."

"Awww, that's unfair. She's single, young and likely lonely."

"Wanna know the tattoo she has on her upper thigh?"

Cranford shook his head. "As it happens, Chief, she may not be with us much longer."

"It was fun while it lasted," Urioste sighed.

"And shame on you, viejito! Es casado!"

Urioste dropped his voice so hopefully Gwenn wouldn't hear. "De verás, Vato? Está bien para tí, pero no yo, eh?"

Cranford flushed crimson, casting a nervous glance in the direction of the kitchen. "Serves me right, Chief. I wouldn't dare show up at Linda Sue's again, but your point is right on target."

The Chief went over to the blinds and looked out. "Diós mio! The snow is really accumulating! So Vato, what do you say? Six months… six months is all I'm asking. Though I'm pretty sure by that time you will realize we support you." He looked anxiously into Cranford's eyes.

"Well, Chief, I've gotta say you really surprise me. I'm willing to recommend anyone for the job you want."

"Beecham brought you here because he thought you were one of the best. His opinion is good enough for me. Urioste Springs needs first class help everywhere, starting with the courthouse. C'mon, Vato, don't make me beg."

Cranford looked down, then scratched his head. "Okay…okay, Chief. Six months."

"I'd also like you to be field advisor for our new S.W.A.T. team. You confident on deadly force?"

"Of course."

"Atta boy, Eddie. Pues, I gotta go. Hasta luego, Señora Cranford!"

"Bueno, el Señor Jefe! Cuidao cuando conduciendo!"

Urioste winked at Cranford. "Tú esposa is one hot chile pepper, Eddie. You hang onto her!"

"It took me nine years to get her to agree to marry me. Puede apuesto I'll hang on!"

Urioste gave Cranford a last slap on the back and was through the door.

Chris and Lupe came out of their room where Gwenn had sent them when Urioste first came. "How come he didn't dress like a policeman, Dad?"

"A lot of top brass don't, Chris."

"Did he have a gun?"

"Probably."

"Did you see it?"

"No, Chris."

"Okay if I tell Denny you saw it?"

"Better not, Chris."

"Awwww."

"I don't think he'd like people thinking he goes around sticking guns in people's faces."

"So what happened, Ed? Are you staying here another six months?" Gwenn had come out of the kitchen wearing the apron she got working for a pizza joint in the capital while still in high school. She always took the apron off when entering her living room. This told Ed she was very agitated.

"I couldn't very well turn him down."

Gwen shook her head. "I'll tell ya, Ed, there's something *very* wrong with this picture."

"Is this one of your *feelings*, Gwenn?" Cranford deeply respected his wife's intuitive feelings. Whether it was who would win an election, or the World Series, when something was coming in the mail or the sex of someone's coming baby, if Gwenn had a *feeling* it was very foolish to bet against it.

"Yes. It was really strong when he first came. He was all nervous and shifty eyed. It was as if he was the wicked queen and I was Snow White."

"And he was bringing a poisoned apple, eh?"

"Yes… he has never liked you. How many times did Beecham tip you off to his rising anger? Your need to be more tactful? All the thousand and one ways you managed to piss him off. I can't see any reason on earth why that would suddenly change."

"Wow me neither." A furious struggle was going on inside Ed's brain. "But *why* tonight's act then?"

"I don't know, but you'd better resign on Monday."

"I can't, Gwenn. I promised the man six months."

"Look, Ed, you don't have to promise to put a gun to your head and pull the trigger."

"I know, Gwenn. I know." Cranford's face was the picture of frustration.

"Okay, Ed, now understand this. I suppose it's best not to pull Chris and Lupe out of school in the middle of the year. Even Stacy is likely better off sticking with Dr. Breckenridge. But come June, we're outta here… with or without you."

"If I'm still alive, that is. Okay, Gwenn, that's fair enough. It's a deal."

"I need another of those cigarettes."

Cranford held out the pack.

Tuesday January 18, 1981: Urioste Springs Police Department; 4th and Alamo Streets

"Back to the fuckin' grind, Hank."

"Roger that, Fritz. I must be ready to retire. When these three day weekends hit, I forget this fuckin' place even exists."

"Boy, I can't wait to be ready to retire."

Urioste laughed. "Any word from the VA?"

"Let's go to your office, Hank."

The top two USPD cops went into the Chief's spacious, carpeted office and closed the door. The Chief's secretary, Ronni Bliss, had the coffee pot bubbling. Strachmann took down his mug from the Chief's bookshelf and poured his third of the day. Lighting a Lucky Strike, he took a seat opposite Urioste's gigantic mahogany desk.

"Dr. Rothman tells me I've a 95% chance of being certified 100% mental."

"You should have done this *years* ago, Fritz."

"Wish I had. Anyway, if it comes through, Hank, I'd like to pull the pin."

The Chief sighed deeply. "Do it, Fritz. You deserve it. By the way, you know I met with Cranford Friday night."

"The bastard's car is still there so I figured you talked him into staying."

"More on that in a minute. He told me, Fritz, that he was left to deal with an escaped mental patient while you diverted his back-up to get Mr. Becker to come get his car."

Strachmann laughed. "Damn straight. I was so hoping that son of a bitch would get killed. I was laughing my ass off while he was calling for back-up."

"Okay…here's what I'm getting at. If you want, I'll use that as an excuse to put you on paid administrative leave while you wait for the VA's decision. Then I'll find your actions justified and you can retire with honors."

Strachmann took a drag on the cigarette. "Lemme think on it Hank." He rubbed his hands together gleefully. "Okay, now tell me about Cranberries."

"He's agreed to stay for six months."

"Plenty of time to get it done. Good job."

"His wife is gonna be tough though."

"Not tough enough. Got it all figured, Hank. We have Mad Dog Mindy tell his wife he was seen molesting Stacy."

"That'll work. She hates Cranford with a passion. He made all her storm troopers write their own warrants. She was livid, but he told her, the cops have to do it on a high school diploma. You've all got college degrees and you claim to be helpless. That's gonna stop now."

"I'm gonna miss that loose cannon son of a bitch!"

"Yeah. He even makes them show probable cause to yank children out of their homes. Mad Dog likes to use anonymous allegations."

"Yeah, so Mad Dog gets her all upset, then takes her to Dr. Broward. He, of course will confirm molestation."

"Well he can't do it physically. So how?"

"He'll tell Mrs. C she showed him on the dolls."

"This is great. But it will never stand up in court."

"That's the beauty of child molestation. It doesn't have to. The accusation alone will drive him to disgrace. Maybe even suicide. He has a history of suicidal depression. He'll never be in a position to hurt you again."

"Good job, Fritz."

"So how did you convince him to stay?"

Urioste shook his head sadly. "One of the hardest lessons politics have taught me is how utterly *lonely*, how *starved for affection* people are. He's got a good job, a beautiful wife, and the respect of his community. You would think a guy like that would be happy.

"But no, he's medicated for both depression and a perforated ulcer."
Strachmann winced.

"So I just puffed him up. Made him feel appreciated. Now we'll put him outta business forever."

Tuesday January 25, 1981: Office of Stanley Broward PhD; All Wars Memorial Blvd., Urioste Springs

"Okay, tell me this," the frustrated psychologist pleaded, "why didn't you just *let him go*."

"Because he could always come back. The man has worked in the capital as well as the Samoan Islands. He's a loose cannon in every sense of the word. The Chief wants him dead and buried and very frankly, Doctor, he's counting on your help."

"A man's gotta live with his conscience, Officer Strachmann."

"Yes he does. But he can live *without* all the court referrals, which is what we've given you."

"The contract was just renewed. I'm sure…."

"Sadly, however, it can always be rescinded if a doctor sexually molests his patients."

"You *know* I don't do that."

"What's your point there?"

Broward just stared at Strachmann, feeling nauseated. "Boy did I make a pact with the Devil."

"Awww buck up, Stanley. Just think of all that good public money rolling in like clockwork every month."

"Okay, Strachmann, I'll do it…and may God have mercy on my soul."

"He won't, Stanley, so live it up now with all that good public money." With that Strachmann left the office.

Wednesday February 9, 1981: The Cranford home…

Ed handed Gwenn her coffee, then lighting a Chesterfield climbed back into bed. A minute or two later he saw Gwenn wiping away tears.

"What's the matter, baby?"

"Ed I'm so frightened."

A yank from his perforated ulcer made Ed put down the coffee. "Oh God, another feeling."

"Yes....an awful dream....something terrible is about to happen, Ed. I just *know it*!"

"Wanna tell me about it?" He moved closer and put his arm around her. As she always did when frightened, she put her head on his shoulder.

She shook her head. "Too awful....".

"I hope it's not the *Tenorio* trial."

Gwenn lifted her head and faced him with tear-filled eyes.

"Oh Ed....I hope it is."

Chapter Five

To S.W.A.T. a Maggot

Tuesday February 9, 1981: State's Attorney's Office; Garfield County Courthouse

"I am keeping my promise keeping these staff meetings to a minimum, but I wanted to express my gratitude for the way you are all pulling together, making me look good."

"We're glad you didn't leave us," Barb spoke up to applause.

"Well thank you. We'll see how things go a bit longer. I still think I'm a marked man and those of you who know the lay of the land around here know what I'm saying."

Karen, Barb, Harry and Marian nodded knowingly…Louie looked down.

"I also want to thank Louie here for the outstanding job he is doing getting the diversion program back on its feet."

"Thank you, sir," Louie spoke to Cranford's nod.

"One reason I was so upset when I saw the results of Marty's negligence was all the people who were cheated out of what might be their only chance to avoid a life at the mercy of The Man. You seem to appreciate this concern, Louie, and I'm grateful."

"My pleasure, Boss."

"Now for some great news. I know most if not all of you have seen the gentleman sitting to my left here during the course of our long and frustrating hunt for a Deputy. Anyway, here he is, from frozen Buchanan County to the far north where he served as Deputy State's

Attorney… a man with over seven years in this stomach-consuming business…Mister Barry Silverman!"

Everyone applauded.

"Thanks everyone. I'm happy to be here. I'll be meeting with the lawyers after this meeting to ensure we have a case selection process in place they both consider fair. Meanwhile, Ed, rest assured I'll be able to pinch hit whenever you need it."

"Sounds like I got just the man I needed!" Cranford said to more applause. "Anybody have something they want to bring up?"

"Just what are we supposed to do with these Social Services people demanding we write out their warrants for them," Paul Feingold asked. "Especially since very few demonstrate probable cause?"

"There's half your answer, Paul. No PC, no warrant."

"They always make threats when we do that. I've never seen anything like this."

"Neither have I, Paul, but my rule remains the same. No one is going to take a child from its parents without probable cause. And no one is going to make you drop all the things you're doing to write out their warrants for them. They're all college graduates for Christ's sake. Our cops have to give us a draft on their high school diplomas. I have no sympathy for those people whose disrespect of constitutional rights is mind boggling. If they give you any shit, pass them to me."

Paul laughed. "Every time I do that they keep saying your days are numbered."

"No doubt they are quite correct. You do not have to take their abuse, however. If they won't see me and won't stop chewing on you, toss them the hell out of here."

It was a good meeting, all and all, Cranford thought to himself as everyone filed out of his office. The attorneys were going to have their first big meeting with Silverman. Karen was doing the Head Secretary job beautifully, and of course Barb was probably the best victim-witness coordinator in the state. In truth she ran the office and had in fact run it for the last three administrations.

He had no sooner settled in and picked up an incoming case file when the intercom buzzed.

"Yes, Marian?"

"It's Mister Weston from Weston's Food and Dairy, sir."

"Okay." Odd he thought to himself. That was where his family bought their groceries. He pressed the button. "Hello Mister Weston."

"Hello, sir. I have some really bad news."

"Oh, what's that?" Cranford managed to gasp as his perforated ulcer reminded him it was still there.

"Your last check was returned, sir."

"It *was*?"

"Yessir, $63.25."

"Oh I'm sorry, Mister Weston, I'll be right down."

"Something else, sir, which is really why I called."

"Go ahead." The ulcer was having a field day.

"That bad nickel Strachmann from the police station was here before the bank called. He was asking if I had any bad checks you had written. I told him no and still said no when he called after the bank notified me."

"Oh my God."

"Something screwy is goin' on here, sir."

"Yes. Mister Weston. I'll stop by the bank first, then I'll bring you your money."

"You know you're good with me, sir."

"Feeling's mutual, Mister Weston."

. . . .

"Well I just don't get this, Mr. Cranford," the nonplussed bank teller told him after trying to find out what had happened, why his check had bounced, for over an hour.

"What was it?"

"Your bank program has been modified. All your deposits have been going into your old savings account."

"But I always use my checking account number."

"That's what's so strange, sir. Our records show that. It's just that your checking ID has been programmed to send deposits to the old account."

"Damn."

"I'm really sorry, sir. Of course we will refund the NSF fee immediately."

"Thank you."

"I'm really glad you came right in, sir. You have about nine checks out there right now that were about to be returned."

"I have a guardian angel."

"We will look into this, sir.

"Thank you, ma'am."

Back in his car headed for the market, Cranford easily recalled what had brought about the political death of the popular and honest Sheriff DeLuca. He also recalled Beecham's warning to check on his bank accounts every fifteen days, this being the interval at which he was paid.

"I'm sorry, Bud." Cranford told the busy grocer as he handed him the money. Do I owe you anything extra for the hassle?"

"No, Mister Cranford. I'll never forget the break you gave my boy three years ago. He's now in college and doin' great....I owe you a lot."

"Bud, junior has more than paid me back. He seemed like a risk worth taking."

"Strachmann didn't think so, chargin' him with five felonies."

"Well as long as I'm around I'll do my best to watch out for everyone."

"How long will that be, Mister Cranford? We keep hearin' that somethin' bad is comin'. Don't take no rocket scientist to figger the chief's fixin to make himself another victim."

Cranford winced with a stab from the ulcer, remembering Gwenn's latest revelation. "Occupational hazard, Bud. I sure appreciate you not telling Strachmann."

"You know, I think I'll regret to my dyin' day not believin' Phil DeLuca. But now that it's happenin' to you too..."

"It's probably only beginin', Bud."

"I've never seen the man lose. If ya don't mind some advice, sir, I recommend you clear out...quick. Much as we really like you. Otherwise...round these parts he can kill you dead as a mackerel without even touchin' you."

"Good advice, Bud. I better get back to the office."

"God be with you, sir." The old grocer gave the State's Attorney a pat on the back before turning to take a shipment of produce.

Back in his radio car, his ulcer tormented him all the way back to the courthouse. *Round these parts he can kill you dead as a mackerel without even touchin' you* played over and over in his mind. Passing the bank, he wondered if he should go in and give Ken Van Meter the chewing out of his life. But naw…his ulcer hurt just thinking about it. All those cases he remembered taking for that fool of a bank president, *making loans of many thousands of dollars, secured by herds of cattle that didn't exist. The man was lazy and stupid. But he figured he had the State's Attorney's Office in his pocket thanks to his four digit contributions to Chief Urioste's war chest.*

Besides, the way they switched his bank codes was probably something that could be easily explained as a mistake. They always covered themselves that way.

Screw it.

Arriving back at the courthouse, a woman was waiting to see him.

"What seems to be the problem, Ms. Martinez?" Cranford asked after the two were seated in his office.

"Well, a while back I went to the law firm I used once before about my husband's failure to pay child support."

"Who were they?"

"Buckley, Meacham & Skeen."

Cranford seldom saw those guys defending criminal cases in court…they were too expensive for the defendants this police department would catch to fulfill their federal statistics. When they did appear, however, watch out. They were tough as nails and well up on all the legalized obstructionism Earl Warren and his cronies legitimized over the decades.

"So what happened?"

"Well, this law clerk came out and told me to take it to your URESA people. Well, sir, I did that and you got me at least part of what he owes and a court order for the rest."

"Glad to hear it."

"Yessir, but today I got a bill from them, charging me $1700 for the work that you did."

"Really?"

"Yessir, I have it right here." She handed a piece of paper over to Cranford. Sure enough, she was being billed for "URESA consultation, follow-up" in the amount of $1700.

"Just a second, Ms. Martinez." Cranford reached for the intercom. "Susan, can you come in here and bring the Heriberto Martinez URESA file please."

"We're just finishing up with Barry."

"Okay, get him to excuse you, please. I have Ms. Martinez in here now."

"Would you like some coffee, ma'am? I've asked our URESA attorney to bring me the file."

"No coffee thanks, I'm too nervous. Do you think you can help me, sir? I don't have this kind of money."

"Depending on what the file shows, yes, I might be able to help you."

Susan Toulouse brought the file within five minutes.

"I'll cut to the chase, Susan. How much time did the Buckley firm spend on your latest activity with Mr. Martinez' arrearages?"

She flipped through the file. "The only activity I show was old Miss Buckley herself called to find out how many hours I'd spent on the case."

He handed the bill across to her.

"Yup… that's what I told her. *Do you mean she can get away with making this lady pay for what we do for free?*" Susan was indignant. URESA cases seldom had legal issues in them, but often were full of frustrating chases to nail down difficult defendants. This was one of those.

Cranford picked up the phone. "This is the State's Attorney calling, I'd like to speak with Miss Buckley please."

"Good afternoon, Edward."

"Miss Buckley. I have Ms. Maria Martinez here with me."

"Oh yes, the woman we arranged a URESA victory for!"

Susan Toulouse was indignant upon hearing those words, mouthing '*you bitch*' so Ed would plainly see it.

"Actually, ma'am the reason I'm calling you is that our records show you were merely a referral."

"Well you better believe, sonny, if it weren't for us she'd have never found the courthouse door."

"Maybe not, but that isn't worth over a thousand dollars."

"Where do you get off telling us what to charge? I was practicing law when you were in diapers, sonny."

"Well, I grew up, and just in time to advise Ms. Martinez that the State provided those services to her for free."

"We've been doing this for years now. All the private firms have."

"I'm sure I don't have to tell you that is fraud."

"Are you threatening me?"

"Not at all Miss Buckley, just telling you and Ms. Martinez that all you can charge under these circumstances *is for five minutes of your law clerk's time.*"

"For a man with no political power base you sure are arrogant. Suit yourself Cranford…your days are numbered." With that she slammed down the phone.

The tug from the ulcer was incessant. "There you go, Ms. Martinez. If she tries to persist, come back to see me."

"Diós te bendiga, Señor!" The lady took her bill and left.

"This happen a lot, Susan?"

"The only one who doesn't is Mister Fine. The problem is most of the people who come to us for help are so used to being stepped on that they don't complain."

"Damn! That is *so* unethical!"

"I think you and Harold Fine are the only two I ever hear say that word."

"Not surprising. Okay, Susan. You heard me today. You should react the same way if this comes to your attention. Just be sure you make a note of any private referral in any URESA case."

"I will, sir." She picked up the file and started to leave.

"How did Barry impress you?"

"Okay. He sure seems to have the political reality of this place down pat."

"How so?"

"He told us to get used to him because he was going to be the acting in two months or less."

Cranford chuckled. "Yeah, he's got it down all right."

Ed Cranford spent the last part of the day in Judge Beecham's chambers.

"Hear you hired a new deputy."

"At long last. Definitely has the qualifications."

Beecham's half smile suddenly had Cranford on the alert. He poured some water from a courtroom carafe and swallowed a pill. His ulcer had been winning too many battles today. It was time to try to calm it down.

"Yes, he's qualified all right."

"Okay…I'll bite, Gil. What's the other half of the story?"

"He's been asked to leave his last two positions because he was working just a bit too hard to succeed his boss."

"From what I've seen of my fellow state's attorneys at those godawful association meetings, they are a pretty paranoid lot."

"That's one way to look at it, Cranford."

"And what's the right way?"

"The right way is at least some concern for the proprietary interest you should have in your position."

"Hmmmm"

"Yeah….'hmmmm'. You manage to signal to all and sundry that you just don't give a shit."

"I truly don't."

"According to the civics book you've got a job to be proud of."

"The civics books don't tell you about a thoroughly corrupt district where one word from a powerbroker and you find yourself *in prison*."

Beecham nodded sadly.

"I dunno Gil how these people do it. I don't think I could take prison, not even one day of it."

"Do you have a plan for coping? You very well might be headed there."

"End it."

"*Suicide?*"

"Well it hasn't happened yet, Gil. I try not to think about it."

"It would only be for a few years….unless of course you just got sense and followed orders."

"I only wish I could, Gil. The problem is I feel I have to be able to tell my Maker that I never destroyed someone's life unless their own actions made it the right thing to do."

"You're a damned fool, Ed."

"Don't I know it. By the way they did the bank account switch on me. Fortunately Mister Weston alerted me both to the returned check *and* the fact that Strachmann was there to pick it up even before Weston heard about it from the bank."

Beecham winced.

"Oh well, another day another dollar. Thanks for letting me know about that."

Cranford had barely picked up his briefcase to leave when Beecham dropped the predictable bombshell. "Don't forget about the other thing I told you about."

Cranford got a major protest from the ulcer on that one. "You mean about Gwenn collapsing on my flank?"

"Yes, my friend. That's what I mean."

"She says she's staying here with me until June."

"Which may be the worst thing that could have happened."

"Can't you shed *any* light on this at all?"

"Something so awful that in the months to come you will know what hell really is."

"But I tried to resign, Gil. Why would he want to do…whatever it is… when he can have my job tomorrow if he just asks."

"I had to figure that one myself, Ed. But what I think, for whatever it might be worth, is that you are on a list for revenge so complete that you will ever be destroyed… never possibly even a theoretical threat to him."

"So you mean leaving wasn't enough because I could always come back?"

"That's what I think."

"Lord."

"Keep smilin', Ed."

"Oh I'm laughin' my ass off, Gil."

On his way home, Ed found himself stopping at Our Lady of Fatima Church. The one he drove Gwenn and the kids to every

Sunday. He went inside, then knelt in one of the pews and prayed until his tears were getting his tie soaked. There seemed to be no solution. The fatal blow seemed so inevitable. It was enough to get the product of a strict Northern Irish upbringing into the church they detested, to beg God for some out from all of this.

At the end of this totally uncharacteristic time on his knees, Ed drove the rest of the way home. He felt a little better, but not by much and even that advantage soon dissolved. There simply was no way out. All he could do was hope it didn't happen, which was about like asking the birds not to fly south for the winter....at least he knew that much.

Saturday February 19, 1981: The Cranford home

The familiar ringing of the telephone caused the familiar distur-bance of the State's Attorney's sleep. Not to mention Gwenn's.

"Hullo…"

"Sir, this is Lt. Burke. We have a barricaded suspect, 400 Block East Railroad Drive, SWAT team has been scrambled. Your presence on scene is requested."

"What's been done so far?"

"East and west ingress blocked off. SWAT team massing outside the house."

"What about to the north?"

"10-4, we'll get a unit to observe ASAP."

"All right, on the way."

Arriving on the scene, Ed saw the usual array of cops in body armor clutching assault rifles. At least seven units were parked, their radios going, their red lights flashing. The B.A.T. mobile, a large one ton truck which the city got as part of a federal DUI grant, was the headquarters. Chief Urioste was inside, talking by phone to the press.

When Ed's attempt to get the Chief's attention was greeted with exaggerated swatting motions, he turned to Captain Haller, the second in command. "Captain get these units on the perimeter where they will be more use in case we need some quick messenger service."

"Yessir."

"Also tell them to turn those radios down. We might have to use them to exchange information we don't want this guy to hear."

"Yessir. Get it done, Sergeant."

Sergeant Washington, one of the better local cops, ran off.

"Okay, how many men here and how are they deployed?"

"We've got the house surrounded, Mister Cranford."

"Yes, but I mean who have you got where?"

"Not sure."

"Well if you are thinking of deadly force as an option you better be sure. Tell you what…. make a tactical diagram of the house and environs, then show where each officer is."

"That's a lot of schoolroom work." It was Chief Urioste, just off the phone, already swearing because his 'light show' had been taken off.

"Chief if you have to order units to move in, you better know where everyone is."

"Ah, you pissant lawyers. Okay Haller get it done."

"Yes, Chief." In no time an erasable crayon board was pressed into service as the men in the truck were finding out they really had no idea where the bulk of their force was deployed.

They soon did.

Cranford stepped out and moved into the darkness, eyes focused on the totally darkened house. He was told this incident began when the angry husband supposedly swerved into the wife's lane as she was going to visit her mother, supposedly never to return. No further crimes were alleged, but when Officer Steele went to serve the citation for reckless driving, the man threatened death to anyone trying to enter. After trying to talk the man into accepting the citation, for the better part of an hour, Steele went to Susan Toulouse and got a warrant for vehicular assault, a Class D felony.

When the warrant service team ran into the same situation, the SWAT team was called out and the Chief took personal command. He had been very pleased upon learning it was a slow news day and all the media of Garfield County turned out. He was enraged when Cranford shut off his 'light show' and pressed his 'props' into undramatic courier duty.

Cranford spent a good thirty minutes, alone in the dark in the February nighttime cold just staring at the house. Trying to put himself into the mind of the poor soul, and that's exactly what he considered him to be, a poor soul. There were several points of contact with his own experience, though obviously this man had gone several steps further. He wondered if his arguments with his wife approximated his and Gwenn's.

Of course he knew that his love for Gwenn would never allow him to threaten her that way, even at his most unfaithful. For him, infidelity had been the experience that took the head off of his anger. It also gave him a sense of guilt that further twisted his self righteousness. He knew Gwenn would never cheat on him in a million years, and the fact she had ways to ring his chimes that a career full of defense attorneys and crooked cops had never discovered still didn't excuse what he did.

But the sad fact was that, having committed to Gwenn for life in all the important ways, including making it clear to the two women involved that he would never leave her, he felt what was left of his youthful nature was quickly drying up, with only a perforated ulcer and his guilt as mementoes it had ever existed.

The working of the action on fifteen assault rifles snapped him out of what he called his self-pity trip. He quickly made his way to the headquarters truck.

"What's happening, Chief ?" Cranford asked, breaking in on a conversation Urioste was having with Haller.

"My men just went on time and a half thirty minutes ago. I'm gonna rush."

"You mean deadly force?"

"Yes. You yourself said we can use with a felony."

"No, I said you need a serious crime *plus* a substantial likelihood that the defendant poses a great danger to the community at large if not stopped by any means necessary."

Cranford became aware several officers were watching this exchange with interest.

"You flunk two of the three outright and have only a marginally passing score *at most* in the other."

"*What do you mean*!!!" the Chief roared, already pissed purple at himself for calling this faggot into his media show.

"Okay… the failures first. You don't pass the 'any means necessary' prong because you can't show danger to the community at large. This guy had a big blowhard exchange for over an hour with two different cops on his doorstep. They obviously didn't feel threatened and the man never left his house since this crime was reported. On top of that, your complaining witness reported this happened with several other vehicles around, yet no one else either came forward as witness to the crime against her, nor apparently felt threatened enough to report a reckless driver.

"For much this same evidence you only make the barest of show-ings on the first prong. Add to it the fact that the man didn't even commit violence in this encounter. He swerved in, then out again."

"That's still a felony, young man."

"Yes, if proven it is. But we're talking here the necessity of a serious crime that transmits the notion of community danger to a prudent police officer. Do you honestly see one?"

"Get ready to rush the house men."

"If you do Chief, you are looking at serious, personal liability in federal court. As are all these men."

A horrible ugly minute slowly dragged by, some ten cops looking first at their Chief, then at the State's Attorney.

"Stand down." The Chief barked, obviously enraged.

"Now… do we have a diagram of the inside of the house?"

"No," Captain Haller immediately answered Cranford's question with a nervous sideways look at his infuriated boss.

Cranford resisted the urge to roll his eyes…to signal to SOMEONE this was a really screwed up operation. As it was, Burke, Haller and Washington clearly were getting the idea, probably knew it on their own, just were too afraid to call the Chief on it. He had demoted a captain and sent him to a beat at Five Points the first thirty days he served as chief. After that, no explicit warnings were needed.

"Can we get one?"

"Yessir," Lieutenant Burke immediately answered. "We have the female half at the station now."

"Good, can somebody get that done?"

"I'm on it," Sergeant Washington spoke up, no doubt viewing the chance to escape the truck with relief.

The next two hours were full of a lot of armed men freezing, a drawing of the residence prepared and an effort by Captain Haller to get Urioste out of his sullen apathy by drawing up assignments for the men if and when the house was rushed.

After an additional forty minutes went by, Urioste began to join in again. It was agreed a heavy tear gas assault on all fire sides would probably cause the man to reveal his position by gunfire, after which the SWAT team could swarm the other three sides.

It was agreed that the forty minutes it would take to make sure no neighbors were in the way and to position the men quietly, in force, on all four sides of the house, would be spent in a last effort to try to get the man to give himself up.

"That okay with you, smartass?" Urioste sneered.

"Do you know where everyone is?" Cranford returned.

"God DAMMIT!" Urioste shrieked."

"I'll try to find out, sir." Haller whispered. Within twenty minutes it was obvious they had lost contact with Officer Johnny Segura.

"He was last seen when we did the initial rush the house deployment," Sergeant Washington recalled.

"Obviously we need everyone to know what's about to happen and we need to know where they are." Cranford and Haller agreed.

"Who volunteers to go find him?" Haller asked.

Several of the men were taking toothbrushes to their weapons, others merely looked down.

"I'll do it." Cranford spoke.

Several of the officers looked up, then furtively eyed the Chief.

"The hell you will," Urioste sneered. "You have no tactical training."

"I was a New Jersey copper when the East Coast was burning to the ground."

"You probably were one of those standing around while those monkeys carried off everything."

"Learn the story of NYPD Lieutenant Gilligan some time. Anyway, I also had plenty in the service and besides, all it takes is concern for the comrade who has no idea what is happening and might well make a fatal mistake if shooting starts."

"Are you calling me a coward?" Urioste drew himself up to his full height.

"I don't have time to waste on you," Cranford returned. "Haller, Burke, you were saying earlier…?"

"I think he might be ripe for a subterfuge," Burke offered.

"Nothing lost," Cranford remarked. "Just make sure *everyone knows* and has their weapons on safety."

"Passing the word." Haller spoke into his headset.

Once again Cranford slipped out of the truck into the dark, then crossed the neighbor's yard and entered the back yard of the target house. Segura was nowhere to be seen. After several minutes of tense, fruitless searching, he noticed the row of bushes that clung to the sides of the house.

Each cautious step toward them seemed the prelude for some deadly fire from the barricaded suspect. *Nope… not yet.* Cranford carefully maneuvered himself inside the bushes, between the hedge and the wall, approaching a window.

No sign of Segura.

There was a sound. Cranford tensed.

Another sound. *Ed was hearing the suspect kneeling at the window right above him.*

Ed kept as still as he could. As usual getting his breathing under control was the biggest problem.

Damn! He could hear the window catch turning…. The son of a bitch is going to drop right in my lap…trying an escape!

Cranford's heart was pounding like the hammers of hell. His .38 special was in his shoulder holster, but Ed decided against it. If the man were truly desperate it might provoke him to fight, with tragic consequences.

He was turning around as he stepped through the frame, coming out backwards. Ed waited until all but his last leg was outside, then sprang. The man let out a frightened gasp, then the two of them went to the ground, with Ed on top.

"Give it up, man….give it up." Ed managed to gasp as he sat on the man's upper torso. "The whole SWAT team is here. Cool it!"

After what started out to be a desperate struggle. The man just gave up. "Aw hell…what's the use. The old lady's destroyed every-thing… everything."

"At least you'll get to live for a better day this way."

"What better day…. Aw hell…what's the use. Fuck it man…fuck it."

Ed stood up, then pulled the man to his feet. "You know, you and I have a few things in common."

"You too, eh?"

"Yeah….come on around with me so nobody starts shooting."

"It would be better if they did."

Ed smirked. "Come to think of it, the best I can offer you is even money."

It was a stunned group of cops with automatic weapons that saw Cranford and the goal of their most recent operation walking around the side of the house.

"Well son of a bitch!" Lieutenant Burke exclaimed. "How'd you manage that counselor?"

"He was tired….just gave up."

Captain Haller got him handcuffed, then had Danny Steele take him to the jail.

Urioste was waiting when Cranford went inside the truck to check on Segura, who had rejoined the group moving around the other side of the house.

"Get this straight you bastard…. I'm in command here!"

Several of the cops who were hanging around the coffee pot inside the truck froze, intently watching.

Cranford was still shaking from the experience. "Let's hope you learned a few things," he gasped.

"The only thing I've learned is to keep you the hell away from my SWAT team."

"Well maybe you also learned to know where your goddam team was before you sprayed bullets all over the neighborhood!"

"You cost me a good two hours of overtime for fifteen men, you bastard. I'm sending you the bill and I want it paid."

"And I want *you* to take advantage of any information available on the inside of a house before you send your men in. It could save several lives. But NOOOO you gotta show how tough you are…"

"You get your pansy ass outta here before I really forget myself."

"That could only benefit this department. Fully conscious you are somewhere between a moron and an imbecile….heading toward the latter!"

Urioste flung himself forward in a rage. Four cops managed to grab onto him. "Chief…come on…"

"I'm leaving, guys. I'll be glad to do a SWAT training Haller, if you want it."

The unhappy captain nodded quickly, so the enraged Urioste couldn't see. As if to tell the enraged State's Attorney that this wasn't the time.

Cranford got the hint, leaving the BAT mobile without another word.

· · · · · · · · · · · · · · · ·

The Chief stormed into the police station after driving at top speed from the scene of the standoff. He ran into Strachmann who wisely avoided the stress of SWAT situations.

"Why the hell is that son of a bitch still running around loose?" he roared. "What's the matter with those pissants at Social Services?"

"No problem with them. It's that jackass of a doctor."

"Broward?"

"Yeah…. all of a sudden he's getting too good for all those crooked referrals we toss him."

"That son of a bitch….c'mon, Fritz!" Urioste peeled out of the police parking lot roaring toward the psychologist's office on All Wars Memorial Boulevard.

"It's after nine, Hank."

"He usually stays late."

"Not *this late*."

"Hey look! Up ahead! That BMW….isn't that him?"

"Will wonders never cease! Gotta hand it to ya, Hank!"

Urioste floored his unmarked police car after slapping the 'Kojak' light on the roof. "I'm tired of this overeducated crook highbrowing us. Who the fuck does he think *he* is!"

"Yeah." Strachmann didn't like highbrows either, and was extra furious the doc had backed down. After all, he was the one sent to persuade him.

Seeing the emergency light, the doctor turned onto a side street and brought his car to a stop.

Urioste screeched around the corner, slamming on the brakes. Before Strachmann could even think of getting out, the Chief had yanked the terrified doctor from his car and slammed him into its side.

"I gave you a job to do and goddam it you're.....!" With each syllable, Urioste slammed Broward into the side of his car. He didn't get his entire threat out before Broward lost consciousness, falling in a leaden heap onto the icy street.

"Damn! Easy, boss!" The two of them stood over the unconscious doctor not knowing quite what to do. Urioste's bellowing voice carried for blocks when he was yelling, and before long over twenty people had put on coats and come outside their homes. This was a black neighborhood, built by those railroad laborers a generation or two ago.

"Should we get a 10-55?"

"Hell, no, Fritz. I don't want him tellin' anyone about this. C'mon!" Urioste pulled on the unconscious man's arms.

"Hey....take it easy wiff dat man!"

"Get the back door open, Fritz....hurry!" Strachmann stepped around their victim and pulled the door open.

"This son of a bitch weighs a ton....he looks so puny."

"Hey man! You be hurtin' this guy!"

General grumbling was going on and gaining volume. Strachmann now reached around and got the doctor's ankles.

Urioste tried to put the doctor in the back seat but low-bridged him on the forehead.

"Dammit!"

"Ain't this a shame!"

"Hey watch what you do!"

"Cops in this town be assholes!"

The two cops finally shoved Broward the rest of the way in. His head and shoulders slumped off the seat. A siren was screaming nearby and getting closer.

"Dammit!"

"Forget it, Fritz. One a' these monkeys musta' called a 55! Just close the door!"

"Who you callin' a….you hear what this honky be callin' us?"

Someone grabbed Urioste from behind and threw him against the car with such force that he tumbled onto the street before he knew what happened.

Strachmann turned around and was promptly slugged by one giant ex-railroader. He reached inside his coat pocket as he fell against the street, only to be kicked by several more, his revolver clattering to the street as he lost consciousness.

Urioste was trying to reach for his weapon, but his hands were too bloody from using them to break his initial fall. Someone gave him a kick for good measure, then the crowd vanished.

"Meet you inside, Roy… if it's safe," a lone white man told his companion as everyone scattered.

The man nodded. "You gonna be okay?"

"Hope so Roy. I can't hide forever with you and Brenda."

"You be welcome anytime, Mike."

"Thank you…. Thank you, both."

The ambulance pulled up to the corner. Urioste and Strachmann were both on the ground. Dr. Broward was inside the back of the Chief's unit, on the floor.

"Damn! What happened here?"

Before Urioste could answer, the lone white man stepped out of the shadows. "These two were beating up on the man inside. The crowd tried to stop them, then Urioste called them monkeys. Then…this."

"Figures. Say, buddy, I'll need your na…. SHERIFF!"

"Yeah."

Urioste was looking at Townsend as if in shock.

"I'll give a written statement on this. I've called the Highway Patrol to take charge of it."

The first state unit arrived just as the ambulance was preparing to leave. Steve Grimes was the responding officer. He gave the Sheriff a statement form.

"Where you been, Sheriff?"

"Here and there, Steve. I'm not used to being a murder suspect."

"Actually I haven't heard a thing about this case since the day he was found shot."

"Everyone was probably waiting for me to show up. I'd like to go visit Cranford. You under any orders to arrest me?"

"No sir. Thanks for this statement."

"Sure. These guys were really beating the guy in the back to a pulp. All we heard was shouting, then the man fell. I hope this doesn't get shoved under the carpet."

"Captain Renfro won't allow that. The rest is up to the State's Attorney."

"As ever. Take care, Steve. I'll see you around."

"You gonna start coming to work again?"

"Yeah....but Cranford will always know where I'm at."

"Okay.... Your statement looks pretty complete. I'll let you know if we need more."

Mike Townsend nodded, then began the short walk to the court-house in search of his unit.

Tuesday February 22, 1981: Office of Garfield County Social Services

"I'm really excited about this, Chief." Mindy Schellenberger gushed to her bandaged visitor.

"It will definitely work for the good of all of us."

"And *especially* the children of Garfield County. Our snatches are way down since that bastard started deliberately throwing roadblocks in our path. What he calls probable cause could cost a child its life."

"Well it's time to get moving on this. I expected the guy to have killed himself by now Mad....uh....Mindy. But everybody's been taking this like some kind of joke."

"Not us, Chief."

Urioste stood up and stretched. "Lemme know the good news as soon as you get it."

"Will do." As the Chief left, Mindy Schellenberger got in her state car and made for the Cranford home.

Gwenn answered the door.

"Mrs. Cranford, I'm Mindy Schellenberger, Director of Social Services. May I come in?"

"You're the people who take kids from their parents, aren't you?" Gwenn studied her with narrowed eyes.

"Not when the parents are such alert people as yourself, Ms. Cranford."

Ed was running a high fever and had been sleeping. The doorbell had awakened him, then the nasal voice of one of his least favorite people woke him up some more.

"I'm afraid I have some bad news, Ms. Cranford."

"Oh….what would that be?"

"I just got a call from one of our most reliable informants…"

"And who would that be?"

"I'm sorry, I'm not at liberty to say."

"Well if you're about to give me some bad news and if it concerns my family, you'd better tell me."

"Sorry, but the good news is I'm ready to take you and Stacy over to Dr. Broward right now…"

"*Stacy*??? What about Stacy?"

"Unfortunately your husband was seen molesting her right at 6:30 yesterday morning. Our informant was walking by your house. Saw it looking right through the window here."

"*Really?*"

"Yes. But as I say, I will take the two of you over to Doctor….HUH!" Mindy gasped as Ed walked into the livingroom.

"Well…well. Mad Dog herself. What's this *bitch* been telling you Gwenn?"

"Language, Ed."

"I had no idea *he* was home."

"Does it make a difference?"

"Of course! This is confidential information."

"You mean from me?"

"Well…no….not from you."

"Well then, what's the harm?" Where her children were concerned, Gwenn wasn't shy at all. Even around strangers.

"Because I wanted to take the two…"

"What has this creature been telling you, Gwenn?"

Mindy held up her hand. "Don't tell…"

"That you were seen molesting Stacy yesterday right through this window, Ed. At six thirty in the morning."

Cranford expected just about anything from anybody after over twenty-four years in law enforcement. But this hit too close to home. He was stunned. He just stood there.

"Lopez! Get over here!" Mindy was signaling her partner to get out of the car.

"That *is* when you usually leave the house, Ed."

"We will take you and Stacy to Dr. Broward right now and get this confirmed, Ms. Cranford."

"Oh *ED!*" She turned again to Schellenberger. "You are absolutely sure it was that time. I'm always still asleep at that time."

"Oh yes….our informant was absolutely certain. Six thirty yesterday morning." Mindy snuck a look of pure vengeance at Cranford. So many chickens were coming home to roost, she could hardly contain herself.

Seferino Lopez came puffing over to join his triumphant boss. Nobody in Garfield County Social Services was going to miss Cranford. The sooner he committed suicide the better.

Gwenn and Ed shared a look befitting their long see-saw struggle of a marriage.

Mindy pointed to the car. "Go get Stacy. We'll wait."

"Well you can just *keep waiting*," Gwenn spat. "I've heard some awful things about you people. I never wanted to believe them, knowing that endangered children pretty much have to rely on you.

"But now I do. And to think that your hatred for my husband caused you to try to use *my daughter* to advance your evil plans for revenge."

"B-B-But…" Mad Dog sputtered. "I'm sure the doctor will confirm this."

"My husband and our children spent the long weekend with me in Borger, Mizzz Whoever- you-are."

Mindy audibly gulped. She had taken too much for granted….was so *anxious* to wreak her revenge….she had gotten careless.

"So you just get on your high horse and beat it before it really sinks in how much you almost got away with doing to my daughter…and her dad."

Mindy wasted not a minute. Seferino was right behind.

"What doctor did she mention, Gwenn?"

"Broward. Oh go lie down, Ed. You're burning up with fever."

"After I take care of this, baby. No way I could relax until I do."

Ed hobbled over to the black Ford and started it up. "Oh Gwenn?"

"Yes, dear?"

"Please call Captain Renfro with the state."

"Okay!!!!"

"Tell him I'm headed for Broward's office and to get me every state cop he can get his hands on!"

"Okay!" Gwenn disappeared inside the house.

Chapter Six

Coming Apart at the Seams

Tuesday February 22, 1981: Office of Stanley Broward PhD

Cranford arrived outside Broward's office on All Wars Memorial Boulevard some fifteen minutes after leaving his house. He was definitely running a fever, so much so that he wondered what was keeping him upright.

No cops had shown up yet and Ed didn't feel like waiting for any. Opening Broward's door, some four people were waiting with their children for appointments. A couple snickered at the sight of him in his bathrobe. Others merely looked away.

"This is not going to be very pleasant, in case anyone wants to leave. Anyone who sticks around for what's about to happen will shortly learn why I am so upset. Some Highway Patrolmen are on the way at my request."

Two women grabbed their children and left immediately.

Cranford knew he should rein himself in….maybe advise this guy of his Constitutional Rights. But he didn't feel like a lawman… he felt like an angry parent.

Less than a minute here and he found himself just getting angrier. Opening the door to the inner office, he grabbed the shrink by his white coat and pulled him out into the waiting room.

"Nora, call the police!" Broward bleated to his receptionist.

"They are on the way right now," Cranford seethed.

"Leave my office right now!" the doctor angrily spoke.

"How does a person like you *live* with himself!"

"Who the hell are…." Broward suddenly snapped. A look of fear came over his face.

"It sounds so impersonal….Schellenberger brings Gwenn and Stacy in, Broward confirms child molestation. It sounds so impersonal, but within that one paragraph is a family forever broken and a child that will one day learn that thanks to your lies, the daddy she never knew either died in prison or committed suicide because of what you quoted her as saying."

Broward couldn't make eye contact.

"This is the kind of thing you do so callously to a child? Saddle her with that memory? With that guilt? Man you are *scum!*"

"They said I would be accused of sexually molesting my child patients. I would lose all my court referrals!"

The two parents who remained with their children gathered them close by, their expressions becoming more and more shocked as they followed the conversation like spectators at a tennis match.

"So you traded my daughter's well being for your crooked court referrals?"

"I didn't want anything to do with this!"

"But you *did it!* Why Broward? What made my little girl mean so little to you that you were willing to perjure yourself? What damn you! WHAT!"

The receptionist was frozen at her desk, seemingly as curious about her boss' answers as Cranford was.

"Urioste and Strachmann beat the crap outta me… said I was going to prison if I didn't cooperate."

"So you hid behind a little girl, were willing to put her through hell to save your worthless ass."

The door to the outside opened, revealing Captain Renfro, Lieutenant Brown and three Highway Patrolmen.

"Sorry, Ed, this was all I could find on such short notice."

"You done good….real good, Harold."

The remaining two parents and their children left by the most direct route.

Ed ran the situation down to Renfro.

"So they were all in it together?"

"Yeah….Schellenberger, this waste of skin here and Urioste. I guess the goal was to watch me commit suicide rather than face the humiliation."

Renfro shook his head. "These bastards have way too much power nowadays. All it takes is an accusation."

"I dunno what we will be able to accomplish, but any one of these people we render unable to function will be a godsend to the people of this community."

"You oughtta see yourself in a mirror, counselor." Harding Carraway spoke with a smile as he led Jill and her photographer, Dennis with his tape recorder and a couple other stringers inside.

"Glad you guys could make it."

"It was worth it just to see the look on your face."

"It's probably just the 103 degree fever, Harding."

"Look at him, guys." Harding Carraway said to Dennis Fields, Jill Mulcahey and the other reporters gathered in Broward's outer office.

"That's not the fever," Dennis said, smiling.

"Nope," Jill added. "It's about time too."

"Well *what* then?" Cranford asked, getting more puzzled by the minute.

"It's the look of a *warrior*, Mister Cranford." Dennis spoke up.

"Yeah," Harding said. "It's a look we haven't seen since you had this job fall on you."

"And all the more welcome for being so scarce recently," Jill volunteered.

Cranford looked down. "You folks are so right. Here I've spent the last two months trying to surrender to all and sundry. I've completely neglected the attitude I should have taken."

"It's good to see it back, sir."

"Thank you, Dennis."

"Okay….so what is happening here?"

Cranford recounted Mad Dog's appearance at his house and what was said, including her gaffe which brought instant smiles. "This waste of skin was standing by to confirm molestation. He was willing to traumatize my daughter for life to protect his contract for court referrals."

Broward again was keeping his eyes on the ground, his face scarlet with humiliation.

"I intend to see if I can destroy this bastard's ability to practice in this state, as well as prosecute for any felonies that might apply."

"Will you handle this case personally, Mister Cranford?"

"Unfortunately, Dennis, my office cannot handle these at all….at least past the opening moves."

"Oh right…conflict of interest."

"Uh huh. But there is still a bit more for you to witness today."

The reporters tensed with excitement as Captain Renfro hand-cuffed Broward.

"Let's pay a visit to social services!" Cranford said with a look at his watch. "We can just beat the lunch rush!"

The giddy collection of state police and reporters set out for the next objective. Grimes listed himself as arresting officer of Broward, but along with his prisoner went to Social Services. Broward insisted he might be of crucial help.

The outer office of Social Services was empty as Renfro, Cranford and the others entered. Mad Dog could be heard clearly, speaking as to a staff meeting.

"Once again, I've got a snatch pool running with Shelly in Newark County. Cranford has definitely set us back this year, but I intend to hit him again and go on hitting him until he commits suicide or goes to a mental hospital."

The shocked expressions on the faces of the reporters reminded Cranford just how case-hardened this evil business had left him. Here he was listening to someone essentially pledging to keep hitting below the belt until he was dead or dying and he wasn't a bit moved.

"Just keep those snatches coming. One thing we might consider if this man continues to get in our way is simply to snatch without a court order. After all we can always threaten the parents with a moles-tation case if they become too aggressive. You can carry the case on your stats as exigency.

"Now Geraldine, Filomena.... Your troubled child multi-placement stats are way down. We promised both Berta Urioste and Samantha Savage at least seventeen foster placements a month, but have not delivered. Remember you can enhance the mix a little by keeping the kid sugared up. Surely you realize that the troubled child grant will get us a new vehicle so let's kick some ass, people."

Dennis Fields and Jill Mulcahey were becoming physically ill listening to this. Cranford's fever hadn't been helped by it either. Cranford signaled to Renfro who blew a whistle causing the social services people to jump with fear.

"Mindy Schellenberger, Seferino Lopez, you are both under arrest." Renfro turned to Patrolman Jack Lawson. "These two are yours."

"On it, Captain." Lawson pulled out two pairs of handcuffs.

Mad Dog noticed Broward standing among the reporters. "If you're even thinking of using that weakling as a co-op I can give you a half dozen times where he engineered multi-placement findings to increase his referral caseload."

Cranford ignored Mad Dog, instead using a social services phone to call his office. "Barb, put Barry on."

"Thought you were on sick leave, sir."

"Me too."

"One moment, sir."

"Silverman here."

"Barry...it's Ed."

"Yessir?"

"I'll cut to the chase.... I have no intention to succeed myself in the 1981 Special Election."

"Yessir...well I'm ready to..."

"You got it wrong, man. They attacked my daughter in our home, so until that election I'm gonna be one unholy son of a bitch."

"Oh?"

"Now you act as my loyal right hand and I'll endorse you to succeed me. Give me any grief and I'll hand you your fucking head. You got that?"

"Yessir. I got it."

"You with me?"

"This comes as a surprise…I didn't think you cared."

"I care."

"Okay then…I'm with you."

"All right. You'll be getting some major conspiracy and corruption cases from the State Highway Patrol. I want you to put those casefiles in 'A number one combat ready order…got that?"

Cranford noticed a couple of the social workers moving toward the exit. "Hold on, Barry…

"Filomena Garcia?"

"Yessir?"

"Geraldine Capehart?"

"Mister Cranford?"

"You two apparently pass for honest around here. Effective immediately, I'm reserving you two as material witnesses. Captain Renfro?"

"Yes, Ed?"

"Book these two into the county jail…have them post a bond with conditions of release. Take them in front of Judge Santestevan."

"I'll give this one to my CIB agent."

"Good idea. You two try to leave Garfield County and you'll sit in jail until after trial…understood?"

Both women were shaking. Capehart answered. "We understand."

"Okay, Barry?"

"I'm here…."

"Okay… Pick a fearless, aggressive State's Attorney's Office with which you are familiar…"

Silverman laughed. "Empty set, sir."

"Okay, then we'll go with Buchanan County. Prepare Appointment of Special Prosecutor documents for each of these Highway Patrol defendants. See if there's anything we can offer them in trade."

"Okay, sir."

"And finally, Barry, notify the state inspector general and social welfare auditors that they need to get down here to deal with rampant corruption in the social services agency."

"Immediately, sir!"

The reporters for the newspaper and radio stations were scratching away madly on their tablets. Their accompanying photographers were snapping photos, while Dennis Fields kept replaying the tape recording of Mad Dog's lecture to her group. All had huge smiles on their faces.

"You've given us our county back, Cranford." Carraway spoke to nods. "It's good to see you in a fighting mood."

Captain Renfro was on the phone to State Headquarters. "Requesting three detectives from CIB and thirty patrolmen."

. . . .

"Because after we take the next step in our State's Attorney's counterattack, we're pretty much going to have to control the streets."

. . . .

"Yessir." He hung up the phone. "Fuck!"

"What is it, Harold?" Cranford asked.

"That was Inspector Johnny Michaels. He is leading a force of ten… count 'em…ten…. Highway Patrolmen."

"Is that gonna be enough?"

Renfro shook his head in disgust. "It's too much, Ed. This is our Tactical Response Team… hostage rescue…armed assault…and so on."

"Damn."

"You've no idea, Ed. That loyal band of newshounds has apparently been flashing this story to Associated Press….and the cable news station. They are *ALL* on the way."

"Okay…I don't want to lose focus. I need to get an Application for Temporary Restraining Order drawn up putting social services in receivership pending arrival of the inspector general and admin types."

"Want me to padlock social services?"

"Can you staff a controlled entry checkpoint for a day or so? I'm concerned about legitimate recipients getting their aid."

"You have me at my limit of manpower, Ed."

"Yeah….forget that last remark. We've got the social workers in jail, so I guess the people still there can police themselves."

The reporters were listening to something, huddled together. It was Dennis Fields who first broke ranks and joined Cranford and Renfro. He looked excited.

"Guess what, Ed?"

"You know it's nice to hear something like that without my ulcer shrieking at me. Go ahead, Dennis....I couldn't possibly."

"We just talked to someone at state Republican Headquarters. They want you to run for Attorney General in November!"

Ed laughed until the other two were laughing with him.

"Captain?" It was the Highway Patrol dispatcher.

"Yeah Sam?"

"That was Strachmann. He says he'll meet Cranford at the truck stop in an hour...provided he comes alone. He's waiting for an answer."

"Tell him yeah." Ed called over. He turned to Renfro. "Can't pass that up."

"I'm not so sure, Ed."

"You worried, Harold?"

"Kinda. We got a couple guys outside the station waiting. Urioste hasn't come out....obviously he's holed up. He has two sentinels outside making sure no state or county cops come in. It's all laid back so far. Still, the man obviously feels threatened. And if *he* feels threatened, you can imagine what that psycho thinks."

"Actually I'm hoping to capitalize on that."

"I'd feel better if we could do a sweep of the parking lot...and at least a look-see inside."

"Okay by me, Harold. I've got that TRO hearing with Judge Cronin at 2:30. I've got Dennis and his tape coming."

"If you get social services declared a nuisance OR insolvent I'll eat my badge."

Ed chuckled. "It *is* novel. But things are happening so fast and we have so few tools to deal with these people..."

"Captain?"

"Yeah Sam?"

"Unit 440 at the county line just reported two cable news station sound trucks and vans. Right behind them were two Associated Press vans."

"Here it comes. I better get lost so I don't miss the meeting."

"I'll have Wesley check the place out. Give us twenty-five minutes."

"Okay, Harold. Thanks."

The Highway Patrol captain smiled. "We can't afford to lose you."

Driving east from the Highway Patrol District Office, Cranford noticed people massed at street corners from the housing project all the way to Alamo. Obviously the people already knew they were going to be 'on TV'.

The Arco Truck Stop

The welcome smell of coffee and tobacco, the friendly clatter of flatware and dishes colliding relaxed Cranford as he stood inside the dining area looking around.

"Mister Cranford?"

Ed turned around and found himself looking at a tall, lean trucker wearing a cowboy hat and down vest. "Yes?"

The trucker smiled. "You don't remember me....do you?"

"Uhhh....?"

"We go wayyyy back, sir."

Much as he tried, Ed couldn't remember. In his twenty-four years at the Bar he had handled so many cases.

"It was eighteen or so years ago.....in a trailer park on the..."

An image flickered across Ed's mind. "On the outskirts of the capital!" Ed snapped his fingers. "Yeah... the big blowout.... With all the guns."

"Yeah....fed up with life...saw maggots in my food."

"*Now I got it!* You're Mark Keyes!"

"Yessir. Well, when you heard I was a Vietnam vet, you recommended me for the VA in-patient PTSD treatment instead of prison." Tears were starting to come to the trucker's eyes.

"Yeah...yeah. Now I remember. You look so *different*....no *wonder* I couldn't place you!"

"Anyway, sir, I just wanted to thank you for giving me my life back."

Both men were misty-eyed as they shook hands. Keyes stuck his logbook in his waistband, gave Cranford a final smile and was through the door.

Every now and then, Ed would get reminders like this one. Reminders of a job well done... of salvaging a worthwhile human life.

Every now and then....

With a heavy sigh, the State's Attorney renewed his search for Strachmann.

Way in the back he was, as if he considered himself the fugitive he should have been for the past decade.

"Hey, Pantywaist."

Those reminders never lasted very long. For every Keyes it seemed there were two Strachmanns....maybe five.

Cranford took the seat opposite, ordered coffee from the waitress on the fly, offered a Chesterfield to Strachmann then lit them both up.

"You'll never get away with this, Cranford."

"Why did you want this meeting?"

"The Chief and I been in tougher scrapes than this."

"Next irrelevant thing you say, I'm outta here."

Strachmann paused in his prepared message, as if taking the measure of his opponent. Cranford returned his stare, all the while taking satisfied drags on the Chesterfield.

"Okay, tough guy... what should I be saying?"

"That you realize that VA benefits can be pulled if the recipient has a felony. That right now getting your pension and pulling the pin would probably save your life. So you would like me to tell you what I need and when I want it."

Strachmann's stare became as hard and cruel as he could make it.

"Don't forget, Fritz...one more irrelevant thing."

"You son of a bitch. You'd really fuck with my pension?"

"With a smile."

"You really think I'd rat on Hank?"

Cranford stood up and tossed a buck on the table for the waitress. "No, but it was worth a peek."

He started to leave, then stopped and turned around. "Oh...just for your information....the Highway Patrol's Tactical Response Team will be coming tomorrow. So call me from the jail if you change your mind. But, as always, each time you waste my time...the price goes up."

"Hey...wait a minute!"

Cranford had gone about ten yards when he heard Strachmann yelling. He just kept going.

Friday February 25, 1981: Courtroom of the Hon. Eric G. Cronin; Division II Superior Court

"This is the time set for the hearing on the State's Motion to declare the Garfield County Social Services Office a public nuisance and appoint a receiver." It was all Judge Cronin could do to keep from rolling his eyes. The novelty of the whole thing was stunning almost to the point of ridiculous. But Cronin liked Cranford. They had tried some complicated cases with complicated issues and Cranford had protected the record through an appeal and several habeas petitions. Judges liked lawyers like that, so he was prepared to cut him some slack when he needed it.

The courtroom was packed. The cable news station was there. The Associated Press was there. Harding Carraway was having a ball, his newspaper was playing host to the twenty-four hour news station's crews. For today's hearing, the TV station was broadcasting from outside the Garfield County Courthouse. Gwenn was positively thrilled when her mom called to say they had watched Ed's press conference on the news station. The whole town was upside down...a holiday mood prevailed.

Urioste was still holed up in his palatial office inside the police station. Inspector Michaels had yet to arrive with his assault team. Some legislators who owed their careers to Urioste had managed to delay their deployment for the balance of the week by filling the Governor with food for thought. That had been digested, and after a short telephone conversation with Ed, the Governor again gave Michaels the green light. They were coming tomorrow.

The cable news station was taping the entire hearing. Parts of it were going to be played on one of their weekend news analysis shows. The cameras were rolling as Ed stood up at his table.

"May it please the Court. I was hoping this proceeding would have been mooted by the arrival of the state inspector general and social service auditors from the capital.

"Unfortunately, it appears the only action they have taken was to bring their attorney at the state level from the Attorney General's Office to try to block the relief we are requesting. We pointed out evidence of widespread corruption, but were told that federal grant compliance monitors were the only people really able to make a decision since it was all federal money involved.

"We are sufficiently horrified by what we saw operating there that we have appointed a special prosecutor who is taking the criminal cases to the Garfield County Grand Jury next week. So if they want to hide behind the usual bureaucratic vaporlock, so be it. We are going to clean this mess out to the very best of our ability.

"Today's proceeding, unlike the criminal case, addresses not the past, but seeks to protect the people of Garfield County in the present and future. Naturally when the state level agency cleans things up down here, we will be happy to withdraw both a finding of nuisance and the appointment of a receiver. But as we believe the evidence will show, the present group at the county level are totally unfit to care for the children of Garfield County.

"The state calls Dennis Fields to the witness stand Your Honor."

Dennis was dressed in a new suit especially bought for this occasion as he made his way to the stand and was sworn.

The usual identifying questions were asked by Cranford… name, address, employer.

"Were you employed by radio station KOJO on February 22, 1981?"

"Yes sir."

"Were you performing the duties of a news correspondent at approximately 11a.m. on that date?"

"Yes sir."

"What, specifically, were you doing?"

"I was accompanying the Highway Patrol and State's Attorney in a raid on Garfield County Social Services."

"What did you understand the purpose of this raid to be?"

"To arrest two of the social workers."

"What happened when you arrived at the Social Services Office."

"The outer office was empty. There was some kind of meeting going on in one of the inner offices. We could hear someone talking."

"Were you carrying any kind of equipment as part of your job?"

"Yessir. A tape recorder."

"Was it running as you heard this voice talking in the next room?"

"Yessir."

"Did it record a tape which fairly and accurately reproduced the voice you heard talking?"

"Yes it did."

"Whose voice was recorded on this tape?"

"Mindy Schellenberger…the director."

"Your Honor, I request this item be marked for identification as State's 1."

"It'll be so marked."

"Now, Mr. Fields, I show you what's been marked for identification as State's 1 and ask if you recognize it?"

"Yes…this is the tape that was running in my machine around 11a.m. on the 22nd of this month."

"Did you have occasion to listen to this tape shortly before appearing here today?"

"Yessir."

"Does Exhibit 1 fairly and accurately contain the conversation you heard at the Social Services Office February 22, 1981?"

"Yes, it does."

"Your Honor, I move State's 1 into evidence and ask that it be played."

"It'll be admitted. You may play the tape."

As usual with such evidence, it seemed everyone in that packed courtroom was anxiously leaning forward so as to hear the tape.

Once again, I've got a snatch pool running with Shelly in Newark County. Cranford has definitely set us back this year, but I intend to hit him again and go on hitting him until he commits suicide or goes to a mental hospital.

Judge Cronin, a born again Christian, was plenty shocked at the notion of a 'snatch pool'. The part referring to Cranford's death or disgrace obviously troubled him deeply.

Just keep those snatches coming. One thing we might consider if this man continues to get in our way is simply to snatch without a court order. After all we can always threaten the parents with a molestation case if they become too aggressive. You can carry the case on your stats as exigency.

Now Geraldine, Filomena…. Your troubled child multi-placement stats are way down. We promised both Berta Urioste and Samantha Savage at least seventeen foster placements a month, but have not delivered. Remember you can enhance the mix a little by keeping the kid sugared up. Surely you realize that the troubled child grant will get us a new vehicle so let's kick some ass, people.

"Court will take a brief recess." Judging from the way Cronin practically ran off the bench Cranford figured he needed to throw up. He was a devoted parent and always took special care in those cases that came before him involving children… especially those without decent parents to watch out for them.

Barry Silverman took over and called Cranford to the stand. He testified to Schellenberger's attempt to make Gwenn think Cranford had molested Stacy, and the reason Gwenn was able to spot it as a lie.

Cranford resumed charge of the case to call Stanley Broward to the stand. He testified he was ready to tell Gwenn Stacy had said, using the anatomically correct dolls, she was molested and her dad had done it. He testified Strachmann had first ordered him to participate and along with Urioste had beaten him up when he tried to get out of it.

Finally, Cranford called Mike Townsend to the stand. He testified to the beating the two cops had given Broward, along with Urioste's verbal comments.

Cranford then rested the evidentiary part of the hearing.

"The Court notes that Assistant Attorney General Pat Johnson, who represents the Department of Human Resources at the state level, is present in court today. This is an *ex parte* proceeding but do you wish to make argument Ms. Johnson?"

"Thank you, Your Honor. There usually are two sides to every argument, but I was here as part of an audit the state agency was asked to perform and thus am not representing the principals whose actions were described today.

"As for the requested relief however, our argument is simple. The public nuisance statute is not now and never has been intended to apply to public agencies. I could easily unleash a parade of the judicial horribles were this to change, affecting police departments, executive offices and maybe even courts.

"I would also point out that as an agency of the state, the Governor could take action as art of general supervisory control, but has not done so. Indeed the state agency itself felt any wrongdoing impacted on federal grants and therefore were properly the province of federal compliance monitors."

Cronin was fidgeting. This was a very bad sign for the person arguing, though Johnson was from out of town and had no way of knowing.

"The requested relief certainly is imaginative, but totally unwise and utterly unprecedented. Thank you."

Cronin was looking at Johnson as if she just landed in a space ship. Too bad the law was so completely on her side.

"Mister Cranford."

"Thank you, Your Honor. Novel, yes…unprecedented, perhaps. But a dark cloud covers an agency in this county that holds the welfare in its hands of helpless children…a class that the General Assembly has found in a hundred different ways is a highly protected class …maybe the very highest.

"I would submit that this argument separates this case from the vast majority of the judicial horribles called to mind by opposing counsel. What may arouse no interest on the part of the law otherwise arouses great interest when children are involved, and whether we are talking of the fraud attempted to be visited upon my family and its heartbreaking impact on Stacy Cranford in years to come, or snatch pools, or keeping the kids sugared up to beef up the troubled child statistics, the disgusting actions of this agency ALL impact on this highly protected class.

"We are very upset by the callous disregard shown toward this problem by the agency at the state level. But we have to live here. And if a tragedy exists that no one cares to supervise, we still have to face it here in Garfield County.

"Courts supervise prisons in many jurisdictions, so obviously the executive supervision argument doesn't survive a showing that the proper actions have not been taken….and they sure haven't been taken here.

"If it is easier to view this as a request for injunctive relief I would simply move to amend the pleadings accordingly. Clearly we do not want supervision of this agency longer than necessary to install a new crew with proper training. But we realize there are many people who depend on this agency for food stamps, utility assistance and so on. And this is why we can't merely abate the problem .

"The State realizes this is a tough call for the Court, but it would be even tougher on children 'sugared up' to the point they are hereafter identified as troubled. So we ask under either rubric that the relief requested be granted."

Judge Cronin, still obviously deeply troubled by the evidence presented, wasted not a minute.

"I'm shocked at the circle jerk game being started by the state level agency here, but that callous disregard for the needs of our children stops right here at the Garfield County line.

"I'm glad you came up with the injunctive relief idea, Counsel, because resort to the nuisance statute was too big a stretch, even though the heartless characters heard from today certainly were a nuisance in every sense of the word.

"The Court finds that the Garfield County Social Services as currently structured constitute a clear and palpable danger to the children of this county. Accordingly the Court will give the state Department of Human and Social Services thirty days to appear and show cause why this supervision should not continue for an additional thirty days.

"The Court shares the concern of the State that those depending on various assistance programs should continue to receive that assistance. The secretarial staff will work with all good faith to assist the Court's trustee in accomplishing this task. Additionally, the state department will arrange for visiting social workers to process additional claims. This will be done at the accommodation of the trustee.

"In view of her social work background, yet independence from the county office, and also because she is an officer of this Court, I will follow the State's recommendation and appoint Susan Toulouse as trustee. She will also report to the Court at fifteen day intervals about progress being made and problems being identified. She will, however, have to sever all ties with your office, Mister Cranford. Will that cause you too many problems?"

"No, Your Honor. We recently hired a Deputy State's Attorney. I believe we will handle it."

"The trustee will be paid the salary received by the current director, adjusted to her longevity in State service. It will be paid by the State Department of Human and Social Services."

"Is the Court's order understood Mister Cranford?"

"Yes, Your Honor."

"Ms. Johnson?"

"Yes, Your Honor. May we ask for a thirty day delay on execution of the order to permit us to take an appeal?"

"That'll be denied. Rout the order through Ms. Johnson, Mister Cranford."

"Yessir."

"Very well. We will be in recess."

As Judge Cronin left the courtroom, Jill Mulcahey, Harding Carraway and Dennis Fields all came up and slapped Cranford on the back, shaking his hand. "You're winning us our county back, Ed!" a thoroughly happy Carraway gushed.

Cranford turned to Renfro. "When are your guys gonna come down and flush out Urioste, Captain?"

"Tomorrow, Ed. I'm supposed to meet with Michaels at 9a.m. and brief the team on the lay of the land. Then they move in."

. . . .

Ed and Gwenn watched the network news out of Oklahoma City that night. Of course they got it all wrong. According to their news story, the State's Attorney's Office had 'taken over' social services.

The cable news station showed several minutes of footage of the hearing, as part of their daily Report from the War Zone, 'where an ambitious state's attorney was today setting his sights on the Urioste Springs Police Department after installing a court-appointed Trustee over Social Services.'

"Is that true, Ed?"

"It was the judge's ruling, baby."

"It's going to be rough tomorrow, isn't it?"

"Yes. The Uriostes have held power here…absolute power…for four generations. I have no idea what's going through that man's mind tonight…neither does anyone else."

Whatever the outcome, the whole nation was going to get to watch it. The cable news station was expecting to have their cameras in position as the Highway Patrol's Tactical Response Team deployed at the police station.

The temptation to do something dramatic was going to be overwhelming.

Chapter Seven

Eye on the Prize

Saturday February 26, 1981: Office of the Chief; Urioste Springs Police Station

Fritz Strachmann walked into the Chief's office to find his boss pouring the latest in a countless series of cups of coffee.

"Dawn is just breaking," Strachmann mumbled as he tried to rub the exhaustion out of his eyes.

The Chief looked up at the portrait of his father in circa 1945 police blues, sighed deeply, then collapsed into his chair. "It's funny... my dad got to retire and rock on a porch for a few years after I returned from Dallas.

"My grandfather was called 'nuestro gran caudillo.' Owning absolutely everything around here, Fritz... as far as the eye could see.

"And my great grandfather...don't even get me started on him. He literally was the nobleman here. He granted Urioste Springs...then called Ojo Urioste as this was Spanish and Mexican rule...its first charter. Can you beat that? The city drew its power from my great grandfather's noble title."

Strachmann nodded. "My people settled in Minnesota... something to do with upheaval in Europe...1848."

"Such a long journey... a long, long journey. Aw hell.... Aw hell." Urioste slapped the arms of his chair as he stood up, then went into his private bathroom. Strachmann shortly heard the buzz of his electric razor.

He knew what was on the Chief's mind. It was the thought process reserved for his lowest moments. How with the death of Hank IV in Vietnam the line was going to end with him. How with his daughter Samantha only being interested in multiple foster placements and his sister Berta pretty much engrossed in the same thing, the long and noble line was truly dead…. Dead because *he* had failed to carry it forward.

Strachmann had been thinking about what the State's Attorney told him. He had been thinking about the possibility of a pension that would finally get him away from the frustration and bitterness that came each and every day of police work.

The Chief shortly reappeared taking a seat at the gigantic desk.

"I don't like the look on your face, boss."

"What's the matter with the look on my face?"

"You look…peaceful."

Urioste chuckled. "Christ Almighty, Fritz. What's so bad about that?"

"Aren't you the one who always tells the troops to stay on guard…. Always alert? That kind of look could get you killed."

"You know me well my friend. As a matter of fact I have some orders for you… special orders."

Strachmann was looking at his boss, positively worried.

"In a couple hours when the sun's up, but before the assault troops get here, I want you to call Cranford…"

"No! Not a ….!"

"LISTEN!"

Strachmann shut up, but his jaw was still hanging open.

The Chief shot him a sharp glance, then continued. "Set up a meeting…then go to it. Tell him everything about the child molestation business. .. at least everything about me."

"But Chief…"

"THEN…. Come back and process your retirement paperwork."

Strachmann was staring at his boss, an unbelieving expression on his face.

"You are gonna get approved for your disability. And everyone and his brother is lining up to tell all about that particular crime anyway."

"You're right there." Strachmann shook his head contemplating the *depravity* of people nowadays.

"So you need to act now, when he may still agree to spare you in exchange for your testimony."

"I can't talk to that…that *pantywaist*."

"We should have never lost this round, Fritz."

"Oh I know. I keep saying…."

"But we overplayed our hand, underprepared our individual roles, and above all, Fritz…" He stopped for a while, looking down, every now and then shaking his head as if deep in an argument with himself.

"I think…"

"And above all…we underestimated our opponents, especially the media."

Strachmann lit a Lucky Strike and took a deep drag.

"You are going to have to live in a world of Cranfords and Cronins, Fritz. Damn did you read what Cronin decided yesterday?"

"The bastard."

"The world is changing….for the worst. I want you to check out of this filthy business…enjoy your pension… get some *peace* in your life."

Strachmann's antennae had gone up at the beginning of this conversation. Suddenly the reason for his instinctive reaction came to him. "You're gonna live in it too…right boss?"

"Oh of course….I just meant I want to see you retire. Maybe for the first time in your life actually feel sunbeams warming your skin… a rose delighting you with its aroma…a songbird charming you with its music."

"Man somethin' is *wrong* with you, boss. You sound like some faggot."

Urioste gave a slight smile, then looked Strachmann in the eye. "Well to put it another way, you saved my goddam life in Korea. I'm gonna save your fuckin' worthless hide now. That better?"

Both men broke into laughter. "Much."

"Glad you're pleased."

The Chief reached for the phone and dialed a number as Strachmann lit another cigarette.

"Father DiMarco? Did I wake you up?"

Strachmann whiplashed to his boss.

"Well you're gonna have to do better than that, Father. Sin has long since been up."

. . . .

"Heh heh… Yeah. Well this is your old sinner Hank Urioste. I guess you know I've kinda' been holed up at the police station."

. . . .

"Yeah… I've been a little remiss there too."

. . . .

"Promise. But first, Father, would you come over to hear my confession?"

Now Strachmann was looking at him shocked.

"Well yeah…kinda soon, unless you wanna watch 'em make a new Highway Patrol training film."

. . . .

"Thanks Father." He hung up the phone. "Fritz so help me if you don't wipe that namby pamby look off your face I'm gonna do it for you."

Strachmann just shook his head.

"Now get the fuck outta here and don't come back without a copy of the statement you gave Cranford."

Strachmann stood up.

"I mean it Fritz. No statement…no return. Now move your ass."

Strachmann's body obeyed, but his face still wore a shocked and even suspicious expression.

"Oh…and pick me up some red carnations, will ya?"

"Yeah." Strachmann managed a smile. "That's a little more like it."

As soon as his only partly mollified number two man left, the Chief walked over to his closet. Opening the door, he rooted through several three piece and double breasted suits, his eyes lighting on his Police Department class A's.

He pulled the old uniform out and began changing.

The Cranford home…

The ringing of the telephone had Ed peering with the only eye that felt like opening at the clock. It was 6:30 and definitely time to get up.

He had told Captain Renfro that he would try to make it over for the briefing. He wanted to meet this Inspector Johnny Michaels, the man who would decide just how much carnage would take place today. He hoped he was wrong but from what he heard so far he figured him for a grandstander... a sometimes fatal disease that would NOT be helped (ameliorated) by the presence of the cable news station.

The cable news station had alerted Cranford that they were hoping for a press conference after the chaos at the police station sorted itself out, a request happily seconded by Carraway, Fields and Mulcahey, three newshounds whose loyalty Ed had come to deeply appreciate.

"Hullo"

"Ed...did I wake you?"

"Oh...Sheriff...I needed to get up anyway. Hey good to hear from you, Brother. I was my usual worried self these past few days."

"From what I've been seeing of you these past few days, seems like you been too busy kickin' ass to worry about one of your problem children."

"You know, Mike...you can't put a brother out of your head."

"I know. Say, Ed, you're really gonna like this..."

"Well then *give* man!"

"Lisa called me this morning. Those bumbling FBI fools *lost* my weapon!"

"Times like this I know there's a God. Do you want a theory?"

"One of yours? You bet!"

"I think one of them did the killing and they realized it might prove more of a millstone than a valuable means to frame you."

"Whoa!"

"Yeah. I think the idea was to remove a potential enemy...you... and a very foolish ally...Moss. I was definitely picking up an unspoken level of desperation that was frightening."

"Yeah...I remember you hinting at that when we were staking out the café."

"Yeah. I also think there's a very negative situation developing between them and Paula Winters."

"Any idea what?"

"No…and as secretive as feds are we are never likely to find out. I picked it up when I talked to her as well."

"How did you manage to develop a friendship with a fed lawyer?"

"We were classmates at law school."

"Oh. Say…wanna hear another weird twist in this case?"

"I'm all ears."

Gwenn got out of bed, signaling to Ed that she was getting their coffee. Ed nodded in response, giving her a swat on the ass as she went by.

"Somebody did a self-help exhumation of his body at the cemetery."

Ed laughed. "Do you hope the body is found or not?"

"Well I'm sure as hell curious as to why it was taken, but I think no news is good news."

Ed smiled to himself, figuring Becker's Automotive was smelling just a little putrid.

"You are probably right. Given the way the frame-up was apparently done, I can't imagine anything that could be found that might help you."

"Do you know something? There was something in the way you asked that question."

"Now now, Mike. Curiosity is for the crime novels."

"Yeah…too bad too. When I used to dream of becomin' a cop, I figgered my natural curiosity was gonna be a real help. My folks always said that with my curiosity I was a natural for this business."

"Oh you're a natural, my friend, but not because of that." Ed looked at his watch. "Hey, Mike, I'm gonna have to get rollin' here pretty quick. Wanna come with me to Highway Patrol HQ? Harold is gonna brief the Tactical Response Team at about nine this morning. This Inspector Michaels seems like a guy you should have in your little black book."

"Sure, man. Why don't I meet you over there?"

'Great…. Say, great to hear from you, Mike."

Ed rolled over and gratefully took the cup Gwenn handed in to him. He lit a Chesterfield and went to work on the caffeine.

"So what you got going today, babes?"

"Lotsa eye candy for the world news media. Likely a big showdown between the city and state on our attempt to arrest Urioste.

"Do you really think he'll ever do a day?"

"Dunno. I'm sure the special prosecutor will move for a change of venue…"

"What's that?"

"It's where the trial is moved to another district because the local scene is too prejudicial."

"I don't think anyone is prejudiced against Urioste here…"

"Right you are. *We* want the change because Urioste is too firmly entrenched here. The special prosecutor is going to be someone from Buchanan County. Now that's as far away as we can get, so I think it's a great choice."

"But didn't you say all those hippies growing their pot up there makes it hard to convict?"

"You got a great memory, Gwenn. In this case that may actually help us. Urioste's an old time cop…and one none too thrilled about civil rights. Now the defense would want Duarte County most of all, with Newcastle County a close second. Both are nearby and both are conservative."

"The whole game is upside down here…isn't it?'

"Good way to look at it."

"Uh…Ed?"

 Cranford tensed. "Oh God, Gwenn… not another feeling."

"Oh Ed…. I'm not sure."

"Huh?"

"You know… I mean like I may not be right."

"Yeah…and apples don't make good sauce. You better give it to me, babe."

The phone rang again.

"Oh fuck…what a time to be interrupted." He picked up the receiver. "Cranford."

"Hello, sir. It's Fritz Strachmann."

Chills shot through Ed's body. His hands began shaking so hard he was barely able to hold onto the phone. "Yes?"

"I've been thinking of what you told me, sir … about my pension."

"All right."

"If you will meet me at your office, sir, say, in about forty-five minutes… I'd like to give you a statement."

"This isn't another waste of my time, is it?"

"No, sir. In fact I will leave it entirely up to you whether you want to give me anything in return."

"That's not very wise of you."

"I'll take my chances, sir."

As Gwenn watched very confused as her husband's face mirrored his inability to figure out what was going on in the head of the man he rightly considered his mortal enemy, Ed finally just agreed to get down to the courthouse.

"I never saw you so… so vacant… as you were just now."

Ed lit up a Chesterfield. "I'm not likely to improve over the next few minutes either. That was Strachmann."

Gwenn just shook her head. "I don't get today at all."

Ed just burst into laughter, then gave his wife a big hug. "I think the day has gotten away from both of us… and it's not even seven yet!"

"Lemme give my dream some more thought, Ed."

"Sure…. Anything to improve that tone of voice I heard you speak earlier."

. . . .

"Here it is." Strachmann handed Cranford a two page statement. He took out a Chesterfield, lit it and began reading.

"Okay, Strachmann, it's all here. I don't know what I will do on the misdemeanor end of things, but I won't interfere with your pension. You will have to testify, of course."

"Oh yeah."

Ed looked at his watch. It was now 8:30. "I gotta run." He stood up.

"Can I take a copy of this with me?"

"Sure." Ed Xeroxed the statement, then Strachmann left with his copy. A few minutes later, Cranford was in his black Ford headed for the Highway Patrol Office.

Saturday February 26, 1981: 4th and Alamo Streets, Urioste Springs

A carnival atmosphere prevailed on all sides of the Urioste Springs Police Station. The cable news station was there, attracting half the town to shout and wave at the cameras. City police sentinels holding shotguns were posted at the door. The Highway Patrol's Tactical Response Team was there, dressed in black combat gear and body armor, wearing black helmets with visors and carrying assault rifles. Their special weapons support was there as well. Behind the barricade of cars on the west side of the station one could see a battering ram, several grenade launchers with the telltale blue canisters already loaded and a flamethrower in the final moments of assembly by an officer wearing a space suit…the suit that enabled a man to walk through fire.

At the far end of the north side parking lot were the VIP observers. Captain Harold Renfro of the Highway Patrol was watching while he talked into the police radio in his car. He had briefed the TRT earlier, then come on scene to pull out his men who had conducted a loose quarantine of the area for the past three days.

Also present and standing next to the Captain, his eyes riveted on the deadly force that had been mustered by the State Highway Patrol in response to his summons, was Garfield County's chief law enforcement officer, State's Attorney Edward A. Cranford. His shoulders were stooped from exhaustion, but his face was alive, practically burning with a new found self-esteem, something tragically missing from the career prosecutor for nearly the last two months.

But it was back now, the State's Attorney riding the crest of exhilaration generated by a noble, courageous assault on the powerbrokers of corruption, cruelty and decay. Every lawman has a limit of the despair he can take before he must swallow his gun or start fighting back. For the past three days Cranford was energized with that righteous anger that only someone watching his life's work being flushed down the toilet can know.

Like he promised, he was one unholy son of a bitch.

Over by the barricade of cars, all with their red lights flashing and radios turned up, the TRT members were shoving magazines into their assault rifles.

"Damn....isn't anybody gonna try to negotiate first?"

"I doubt it, Ed," Captain Renfro answered. "This Michaels is all blood and guts. Never saw a guy less aware of the crap we have to watch out for."

With the metallic snap of the magazines going in, and the louder working of the actions on all the assault rifles a few moments later, the two city sentinels were looking wide-eyed at each other.

The TRT members now shoved their visors down, obscuring their faces.

The cable news station was lapping up the flashing red lights and the squawking of the radios. When half the TRT changed position to the northern end of the cars, so as to have a view of the two terrified city cops, it seemed the world held its breath.

The other half of the team, covered by the first half, moved the battering ram into position. It was a huge spring loaded device that apparently would push the front door in pieces some twenty yards inside the building. Cranford had seen the film the TRT showed at the briefing. He was gasping for breath.

"You two better move. We fire this whether you do or not, in exactly two minutes." A mechanical, nerve grating countdown began.

The local Highway Patrolmen were urging the two to move. The TRT seemingly could care less.

"100...99...98...97...96"

The mob that had been shouting and waving at the cameras were all silently watching the massed troopers....eyes wide.

The battering ram made a nasty sound as it was cocked. Upon hearing that, the two city cops simply ran away from the door, their nerves totally unprepared for this kind of stuff. The local Highway Patrolmen gave a sigh of relief. The TRT still could have cared less.

72...71...70.....69....

A local 'roach coach' had been doing a land office business selling coffee, soup, danishes and hot chocolate. Suddenly all the people in line were turned toward the awesome sight... eyes riveted. The guy inside had come out and was also silently watching.

Now the entire team lined up in three ranks behind the battering ram. This was obviously it... the deadly assault would begin with no opportunities to surrender. Cranford couldn't believe what he was seeing. The TRT was just a mass of black, complete with black assault rifles…all barrels pointed toward the city police door.

52…51…50…49… The countdown relentlessly went forward.

Suddenly the door to the city police headquarters opened. Strachmann, looking pale as a ghost, stepped onto the area where the two sentinels had been.

"Chief Urioste is dead," he intoned in a loud clear voice. "A single bullet through the brain." Strachmann wiped at his eyes, then went back inside.

The two sentinels who had regrouped at the far end of the parking lot just looked at each other, then silently followed Strachmann inside.

Inspector Michaels now stepped out in front of the battering ram. The countdown stopped. The spring was disengaged from its deadly taut position, as half the TRT, weapons pointed forward, charged into the city police headquarters. The other half continued to cover them.

Everybody…absolutely everybody…including the cable news station crews, breathed a sigh of relief….a huge sigh of relief.

. . . .

The high school auditorium was pressed into service for the press conferences of Inspector Michaels and State's Attorney Cranford. The cable news station cameras were filming away as reporters from their network, the Associated Press and the utterly thrilled local newshounds who had stood by Cranford when he needed it most were there to fire questions.

"Inspector, it was sure looking like there was going to be no discussion, no additional warning and no further delay before you set off the battering ram. Did we read that right?"

Michaels smiled. "You sure did. We aren't even called in until the negotiation has proven fruitless. At the end of the two minute countdown the battering ram would have turned the station doors into splinters and would have killed anyone within twenty yards of the impact area."

"Aren't you afraid of liability?"

"We don't look at it that way. We ask are *you* afraid of dying. We find this perspective works better."

"How much longer is your team going to be with us, Inspector?"

Michaels looked at his watch. "About five minutes. We need to get back to the capital and debrief."

The auditorium full of cameras and reporters went silent, the news-hounds looking around at one another. All at once they burst into applause. There was something cleansing and surefooted about this approach.

Cranford came out on the stage next. The local reporters and their crews began applauding, then cheering, then finally a standing ova-tion, which shortly spread throughout the auditorium.

The network people had no idea what was going on, but every local in that crowd sure did. Cranford had very reluctantly succeeded to his office at a time when the Urioste machine held something close to absolute power. Their power was supplemented by a vicious social services apparatus who knew that even the whisper of an accusation was all it took to condemn someone to disgrace.

The power of these two mighty players reached its pinnacle when Mad Dog had felt so comfortable in her ability to destroy even the Chief Law Enforcement Officer that not even minimal preparation was believed necessary. How many lives they had actually destroyed was unknowable, since many no doubt simply disappeared, leaving these people in the driver's seat, even more emboldened for the next target.

Fortunately a few reporters never lost hope in their ability to regain their county, and when the State's Attorney was finally angered out of the doldrums by an attack on his own daughter that misfired, the two joined forces with the Highway Patrol and in a mighty turning of the tide routed the seemingly impregnable bastion of corruption.

All three of these allies were crucial. The State's Attorney had the necessary law enforcement powers and familiarity with the system. The reporters had at least some ability to marshal public opinion, while the Highway Patrol provided a crucial armed force and inves-tigative ability.

"But let's not kid ourselves," Cranford continued with his remarks. "As long as society is rightfully scandalized by sexual assaults against children, people who lack the moral fiber and honesty to use their powers wisely can always gain and hold power with the threat of such accusations.

"As long as the good people of a community desire to equip their law enforcement agencies with sufficient power to effectively combat crime, people who lack the moral fiber and honesty to use these powers in the manner they were intended to be used can always send innocent people to prison with perjured evidence. Can always steal and defraud with virtual impunity.

"We won this round, but only because of overconfidence on the part of an organization that had its own way around here for decades.

"I have made it clear to my wife and to my staff, that twenty-five years fighting the very special type of discouragement reserved for those in law enforcement is more than enough. I will not run in the special election to fill Judge Beecham's vacancy in the State's Attorney's Office, nor will I run, as some very kind folks have suggested, for state attorney general.

"Instead, I will devote the remaining ten months to ensuring that such arrogance of power recently vanquished does not once again take root in Garfield County. In so doing, I will continue to count on those devoted journalists who helped deliver us in the week just past, the loyalty of my staff and dedication to duty of our many honest cops.

"When these forces are combined with an alert and interested citizenry, we cannot possibly fail. And please God this is exactly the type of citizenry we have here... have now."

A tremendous ovation saw the State's Attorney off the stage. Within the succeeding two days, the cable news station and the Associated Press would be leaving, leaving behind a citizenry that for a few giddy days one week in February had truly bonded with one another and with their public officials to put an end to the atmosphere of apathy and pessimism that a political machine ever needs to steal a people's birthright.

THE END

Police Radio Ten Code

Police radio codes vary in different places and over time. Here is the one used in the book.

10-4	Acknowledge; okay; will do
10-5	Relay
10-6	Busy, unable to take traffic
10-7	Out of service; dead
10-8	In service
10-9	Repeat
10-10	Out of service, subject to call
10-12	Visitors present; could refer to spouse or significant other
10-15	Prisoner; person in custody
10-19	Return(ing) to station
10-20	Location?
10-21	Call _____ at _____
10-22	Disregard; take no further action
10-23	Stand by
10-24	Officer needs help (very serious)
10-28	Motor vehicle registration check
10-29	Check for warrants
10-33	Emergency
10-42	Officer at home; home or residence
10-44	Accident without injuries
10-45	Accident with injuries
10-48	Armed and dangerous
10-55	Ambulance; ambulance requested at _____
10-61	Officer injured at _____

10-76	Officer enroute
10-80	Use caution
10-87	Meet
10-97	Officer at scene
10-98	Finished; last assignment completed

Glossary of "Insider Talk"

Here are some of the slang or insider terms used in this book

<u>UC or "undercover people"</u>----while this sometimes can mean a police officer, as used here it means convicts the FBI breaks out of state prison to make buys for them.

<u>Reverse sting</u>----where law enforcement sells drugs to supposed dealers, then arrests them for possession.

<u>Discovery or discovery laws</u>---The rule of criminal procedure that lists information the state must disclose to the defense in advance of trial.

<u>Rap sheet</u>---document listing a person's criminal record.

<u>Letting [a drug] walk</u>---In a reverse sting, refers to the drugs law enforcement sold to a supposed dealer.

<u>Accessory charges</u>---Charges for assisting a person committing a crime; in many states punishable to the same extent as the crime.

<u>OJT</u>---on the job training.

<u>Sting op</u>---operation where one officer buys from a pusher and others make the arrest; sometimes on the same day, other times after fifty or more buys are made all over the jurisdiction and there are mass arrests on warrants.

<u>ASAP</u>---as soon as possible.

<u>P.O.</u>---probation officer

<u>B.A.T. mobile</u>---vehicle equipped with Breath Alcohol Testing [BAT] apparatus.

<u>S.W.A.T. Team</u>---Special Weapons And Tactics team.

<u>Co-op</u>---as used by Schellenberger in chapter 6 it means 'co-operating witness', referring to a potential defendant who for a promise or guarantee on charges or disposition [sentence received] is testifying for the State.

<u>Material witness</u>---witnesses who have highly relevant testimony but who are identified as potential flight risks. Depending on the state's statutory provisions, they may be subject to imprisonment in lieu of posting sufficient bail to be released on conditions.

<u>TRO</u>---temporary restraining order. First step in getting injunctive relief. Order is good usually for ten days after which a hearing with notice to all parties is held.

Free Translation of Spanish Words in Chapter Three

"Jefe cuidao!" Gwenn barked—*careful, Chief*

"¡Queremos volver a la casa de mis padres!"—*we want to return to the house of my parents!*

"Señora Cranford… quienes son *nosotros* ?"—*Mrs C, who are "we"?*

"Yo y mis hijos…los tres." *Me and my kids…the three.*

"No se preoccupe, Señora. Su esposo, sus niños y usted será bastante bien."—*don't worry, ma'am….your husband your children and yourself will be just fine*

"Ojalá qué sí el Señor Jefe."*may God grant it Chief*

"And shame on you, viejito! Es casado!"-*old man. You are married*

"De verás, Vato? Está bien para tí, pero no yo, eh?"-*oh really,bud….it's okay for you but not for me, eh?*

"Pues, I gotta go. Hasta luego, Señora Cranford!" *until later Mrs Cranford.*

"Bueno, el Señor Jefe! Cuidao cuando conduciendo!"*okay, Chief… careful wh0ile driving.*

"Tú esposa is one hot chile pepper, Eddie. You hang onto her!"*your wife*

"Puede apuesto –*you can bet*

This translation was requested by my brother in Wales, Lee Bridge

About the Author

John W. Cassell was born in Baltimore, Maryland in 1948, underwent primary and secondary schooling in Pennsylvania and New Jersey, graduating from the University of New Mexico with a degree in political science in 1969. His first job was with an Atlantic City, NJ radio station where he was a disc jockey as well as a copy and news writer. He worked for a consortium of Pennsylvania and New Jersey radio stations as a floor correspondent at the 1964 Democrat National Convention.

In August of 1969 he traveled to Europe, hitchhiking from Holyhead in Wales to Algeciras in the south of Spain. He then traveled as well in North Africa. Following his return to the United States, he traveled around the country for a year, working as a truck driver, dishwasher, postman, factory hand and other blue collar jobs until 1973 when he enlisted in the United States Air Force, serving with the Strategic Air Command until June of 1976.

He entered the University of New Mexico School of Law in 1977 on the GI Bill and was awarded his Juris Doctorate *magna cum laude* in December of 1980. Since that time he served with the New Mexico State Police as well as the New Mexico Attorney General and District Attorney offices in different parts of the state. For over ten years and until disabilities connected with his military service compelled his retirement in 2006, he worked as a trial prosecutor in the Samoan Islands.

Cassell now lives quietly in the American Southwest with his beloved wife of 32 years. The couple has five children, six grandchildren and one great grandchild.

His first feature length book, SOLDIER OF AQUARIUS: 1969-1970 was written in 1976 upon discharge from military service. While resident in the South Sea Isles, from 2001 until his retirement, Cassell wrote some six other feature length books in various genres.

CPSIA information can be obtained at www.ICGtesting.com
Printed in the USA
BVOW032353040412

286821BV00002B/82/P

9 781592 997398